ESSAYS ON BETA, VOL. 1

Niels Pflaeging

ESSAYS

NIELS PFLAEGING

ON

BETA,

VOL. 1

WHAT´S NOW & NEXT
IN ORGANIZATIONAL
LEADERSHIP,
TRANSFORMATION
AND LEARNING

BETACODEX PUBLISHING

OTHER TITLES FROM BETACODEX PUBLISHING:
Volume 1. Niels Pflaeging: Organize for Complexity, 2014
Volume 2. Silke Hermann I Niels Pflaeging: OpenSpace Beta, 2018
Volume 3. Niels Pflaeging I Silke Hermann: Complexitools, 2020

Cover & book design: Esra Oezen, Niels Pflaeging
Cover photo: Aron Süveg
Illustrations: Pia Steinmann, pia-steinmann.de
Additional illustrations: Niels Pflaeging
Additional translations into English: Bjoern Janssen
Copy editors: Andi Roberts, Matt Moersch, Paul Tolchinsky,
Steve Holyer

ISBN 978-3-948471-00-2 (print)
ISBN 978-3-948471-01-9 (ebook)

Visit our websites: www.betacodexpublishing.com I
www.redforty2.com I www.nielspflaeging.com I
www.openspacebeta.com I www.betacodex.org

INDEX

A foreword. By Silke Hermann   8

What is Beta?   10

Why we cannot learn a damn thing from   18
Toyota or Semco

OrgPhysics. The 3 faces of every company: 26
How a triad of structures allows
companies to absorb complexity

Flat hierarchies: They are just another   38
step in the wrong direction

Change-as-Flipping:
Change is more like adding milk to coffee   44

Your company has exactly the culture it deserves   54

Abolish bonuses! There is no way around that   60

Bye-bye Management by Objectives!   66
From fixed to relative performance

Social Density: The key to self-organization   76

Competition in organizations: 82
Is it good, or is it bad?

The McGregor Paradox. The most tragic misunder- 88
standing in the history of work and organizations

Five secrets of Very Fast Organizational   92
Transformation (VFOT)

Leadership styles: They are not   108
what you think they are

Bosses vs. leaders: Companies need neither!   112

Crazy. Stupid. Learning. The 2 types   118
of learning and why both matter

Thinking tools: Management vs leadership   124

Differences that make a difference   126

7 reasons why the   132
digital transformation is over-hyped

Heroes of leadership: Three "founders"   138
of organizational leadership, acknowledged

Thinking tools: Organizational Hygiene   144

Overview of sources, recommended reading   146
About the author   150

A FOREWORD.
BY SILKE HERMANN

This collection of essays unites 20 texts by Niels, written between 2014 and 2020. You will find that the texts in this book are diverse both in terms of style and topics. They are of wildly different character and length, too: Some highly conceptual, some more essayist in nature. But we are sure you will find them to be crisp and entertaining.

Topic-wise, this little book covers quite lot of ground. It touches everything from the history of leadership to learning; from organizational design to performance systems; from transformation method to digital transformation; from philosophy to the role of language. The one thing all 20 articles have in common is that they all relate, in different ways, to what is Now and Next in the world of work and organizations.

Between 2014 and 2020, two things occurred. Niels expanded on themes which had already been touched upon in his award-winning books from 2006 and 2009, *Leading with Flexible Targets* and *The 12 New Laws of Leadership* (both as yet unpublished in English). Examples of this are the essays on *Relative targets* (page 66) and *decentralization* (page 38) in this volume. In addition, Niels and I started to develop and articulate entirely new concepts, together. Some of the more conceptual pieces in this book are testament to these more recent additions to the ever-evolving BetaCodex canon. Texts on *OrgPhysics* (page 26), on *Change-as-Flipping* (page 44) and on *Very Fast Organizational Transformation* (page 92), are examples.

In 2008, just after leaving the Beyond Budgeting Round Table think tank, Niels founded the BetaCodex Network. Together with colleagues from Brazil and Germany, he saw this new network as an attempt to start an open source movement that would help turn Beta into "the standard organizational codex" in the world, sooner or later. While we are still far off in fulfilling that vision, we can rightfully say that collective consciousness has already shifted towards a clearer understanding of organization-wide self-organization, decentralization and democracy. The tireless work done by Niels and others in the BetaCodex community to promote the practical theory of Beta, and the ideas presented in this book have certainly contributed to that mind-shift.

Niels has published most of the articles in this volume on-line (see "Overview of sources"). With this book, we are making these thought-provoking, timeless essays accessible to a larger audience, in a delightful, highly engaging format. For this book, all texts have been carefully reviewed, updated and, where necessary, somewhat enhanced. Finally, two of the articles are entirely new translations of essays by Niels from German. They are being published in English here for the first time.

I hope you enjoy browsing and reading this book! It might inspire you to act in Beta, too.

Silke Hermann, August 2020

SO WHAT IS "BETA" ALL ABOUT?

The BetaCodex is not for "some." It is for all organizations. Large or small. Long-established or start-up. Local or multi-national. Profit-oriented, not-for-profit, or public service. Why?

In order to address complexity, organizations do not need one monolithic tool or theory: They do not need a framework. Instead, they need coherent, shared language and imagery, and a "system of systems" concept that everyone in the organization can acquire and integrate through learning.

Consequently, it is crucial to Beta that it is not based on rules, but on principles. Unlike other organizational concepts, the BetaCodex is neither a prescription nor a hammer, nor is it a one-size-fits-all solution. It is a system of systems concept, a way of thinking and acting, a way of being.

The difference between rules and principles is that for setting up rules, you need to analyze every possible situation before formu-lating it. Rules are based on the pattern of *if-this-happens-do-that*. Whenever a previously unknown or unthinkable situation occurs, however, rules fail. That is like landing on the Hudson River. Rules simply do not support you in finding good solutions to never-before-thought-of problems. Surprising problems, however, now occur regularly in our everyday work lives and in our businesses.

Principles vs. rules: They are not the same. This distinction matters!

Principles, by contrast, do not just apply to known problems. You do not need to be aware of all possible situations. You apply them within whatever situation as it occurs. Principles are like guidelines that help you test whether your actions are aligned with your be-

---

THE LAWS OF BETA (DO THIS!)
versus the Laws of Alpha (Not that!)

LAW	DO THIS!	NOT THAT!
01. Team autonomy	Connectedness with purpose,	not dependency
02. Federalization	Integration into cells,	not division into silos
03. Leaderships	Self-organization,	not management
04. All-around success	Comprehensive fitness,	not mono-maximization
05. Transparency	Flow intelligence,	not power obstruction
06. Market orientation	Relative Targets,	not top-down prescription
07. Conditional income	Participation,	not incentives
08. Presence of mind	Preparation,	not planned economy
09. Rhythm	Tact & groove,	not fiscal-year orientation
10. Mastery-based decision	Consequence,	not bureaucracy
11. Resource discipline	Expedience,	not status-orientation
12. Flow coordination	Value-creation dynamics,	not static allocation

liefs and values, or not. If not, you have to search for another way to solve the problem. Understanding this difference, you are able to adopt BetaCodex principles (or "laws") to your firm or to situations you encounter at your work – anywhere, at all times. Still, we have recognized that it takes practice to understand the full impact of the BetaCodex, as compared with tayloristic organization. This is because the model is based on a set of 12 cohering and interdependent principles (shown on the left). Only when applying the full set of principles will your organization be rewarded with the superior results the codex offers.

THE TROUBLE WITH ALPHA:
IT DIED A PRETTY LONG TIME AGO

The BetaCodex is the alternative to command-and-control, or the social technology commonly referred to as management – or Alpha, as we often call it. Sadly and inappropriately, Alpha is the organizational way of thinking and acting upon which most organizations are still built today. Alpha became a "zombie technology" when the industrial age ended, around four decades ago. In a way, Alpha stopped making sense – and hardly anybody noticed. Or everyone noticed, and nothing changed, nevertheless. Fact is: Alpha remains the default organizational model of our time. The *zombification* of Alpha, or management the social technology, has not stopped organizations from applying its principles, its methods, and its image of human nature. Organizations today are "stuck" in command-and-control mode. We are habituated, addicted to an old frame of reference. That is the bad news.

The good news is twofold. Firstly: this will change, over time, due to the inescapable forces of complexity. Secondly: The alternative to Alpha already exists in quite a few, diverse organizations around the world. This is where Beta comes into play: Beta is the contemporary organizational codex for today´s complex world. Beta, much different than Alpha, is not just fit for complexity, but also fit for human beings as they are. This is why Beta will prevail and become the standard organizational codex.

The 12 laws of the codex articulate a coherent new organizational model that is opposed to the command-and-control management model which thought leaders like Frederick Taylor, French engineer Henri Fayol, automotive executives Alfred Sloan and Henry Ford developed about 100 years ago. The principles of Beta are not a salad bar to choose from: You do not get to pick the principles you are most comfortable with! Only by applying the full set of the 12 principles are organizations rewarded with the superior performance the model has to offer. Lennart Francke, former CFO of Svenska Handelsbanken, was often asked if the Handelsbanken model, today known as the Beyond Budgeting model, could be applied partly, in bits and pieces, and he replied: "Imagine Great Britain would change from left-side traffic flow to right-side traffic as practiced on the European continent. And imagine that the British people might say: 'Okay, but to us, the British, that appears way too radical and too complex to be done in a rush. Let´s therefore start next week with the buses and the trucks only.' It is just the same with Beyond Budgeting."

To describe the new breed of post-tayloristic 21st century organization, which we call "BetaCodex" organizations, these expressions fit well: *decentralized, or "devolved," adaptive, agile, ethical, people-oriented, empowering, entrepreneurial, democratic, lean, market-driven, complexity-robust, sense-and-respond, un-bureaucratic, networked, sustainable*

Since 1998, the Beyond Budgeting Round Table (BBRT) and then its spiritual successor, the BetaCodex Network, have drawn upon case study-based research to conclude that companies with a contemporary view of human nature don't control them with plans and fixed targets, but rather they aim for "relative" performance contracts with them instead. Early on, the BBRT concluded that there had to be a set of 12 central principles of the organization model based on "relative performance contracts," contrasted against the assumptions of fixed performance contracts.

Relative performance contracts (which we will explore later in this book, see page 60) are based on the assumption that it is unwise to set fixed targets for managers and teams and then try and control their behavior and activities in terms of these targets. The implicit agreement is that it is the task of managers to provide an inviting, stretching and open work climate within which employees agree to aim for continuous performance improvements. Managers and employees collectively use their knowledge and their own common sense to adapt to changing conditions and environments.

With relative performance contracts, decisions are not made at the top. Instead, they are distributed, decentralized, and devolved as far out as possible. This type of performance contract is based on mutual trust. Increased transparency and higher expectations towards teams (compared to competitors or their equivalent), provide a permanent challenge. Responsibility for performance and decision-making are gradually moved away from individuals in the center of the organization towards teams in the periphery.

THE BETACODEX:
A MINDSET, A MENTAL DISCIPLINE, A PHILOSOPHY

The BetaCodex suggests another way of looking at performance, success, and an organization´s raison d´être. Ask yourself: "Why does your organization not deliver the performance you might expect?" Or: "Why does performance not improve?" Or: "Why do people in your organization seem de-motivated?" Well, then, the BetaCodex suggests, you should ask for the causes not by assigning blame, but by identifying the systemic problems in the organization itself. Systems theorist W. Edwards Deming once stated that about 95% of all problems within organizations are caused by the system, and only 5% by humans within the system. He had a point.

FROM BEYOND BUDGETING
TO THE BETACODEX

The BetaCodex is a "mind set" that results in putting an end to taylorism and hierarchical command-and-control. Through decentralization, it allows to shift entire organizations to total market-pull. In this sense, the organization can become "managed," or steered by market-pull, instead of relying on internal steering. Traditional "management" and "governance" become obsolete. If they continue exist, they are counterproductive, lead to waste and can even harm the organization.

While the origin of this thinking is the so-called "Beyond Budgeting model," our research between 1998 to 2007 taught us that the term Beyond Budgeting led to some confusion. We saw countless academics and "experts" fall prey to the idea that a concept by that name had to be somehow related to "planning," or finance management. In our views, the term "Budgeting" in Beyond Budgeting merely hinted at the starting point that the movement had departed from: Many other starting points would have been possible.

The transformation proposed by the Beyond Budgeting model and movement could have been appropriately described through the Peter Drucker phrase that *"90% of what we call management are actually practices that keep back people from doing their work."* The challenge is to abolish those 90% of management practices and get the 10% of actual leadership practices right. Although "Beyond Budgeting" was never conceived as a controlling or financial concept, even publications from acknowledged management experts proved that the term Beyond Budgeting was all too often misunderstood. Therefore, we finally re-baptized the Beyond Budgeting model as "The BetaCodex," in 2009.

FOUNDATIONS OF THE BETACODEX
BASED ON PRACTICE, FIRMLY ROOTED IN PRACTICAL THEORY

The rise of the new organizational model that we call the BetaCodex is driven by today's ever-changing world. No less. Today's dynamics and uncertainty defy industrial-age wisdom of "management" and organizational design. The 100-years old notions of managing do not support today's critical success factors which are more varied than in the industrial age. The command-and-control management model is insufficient for the 21st century precisely because of that.

The BetaCodex itself is supported by two pillars. First, by scientific thought leadership from fields as varied as complexity theory, psychology and the business sciences. Second, it is supported by practice – through pioneering organizations of varying history, size, cultural background, and from vastly different industries. The case for change is so compelling today, because now, theory from different sciences, and practice from pioneering organizations which are leaders in their respective fields, come together. In one, robust organizational theory that is the BetaCodex.

WHY WE CANNOT LEARN A DAMN THING FROM TOYOTA OR SEMCO

The future of work is already here. And not only in the minds of some outstanding thinkers, high-minded idealists, quirky innovators and lofty utopians – or people like you who are reading this book! No, the future of work and organizational leadership is tangible. It is out there in the real world: You can find it in the practice of at least a few dozen extraordinary, pioneering organizations that have cracked the code, solved the puzzle, and removed all doubt. I'm talking about "the Toyotas" of this world. The W.L.Gores, the Southwest Airlines, the Googles, the Handelsbankens, the Semcos. Companies like these have been doing things differently for 20, 30, 40 or even 50 years, in the case of Toyota. *Yeah, we heard all that before,* you say? Then let me ask you: *What have we really learned from those incredibly great companies?*

For over 15 years, I have researched, thought, spoken and written about what I like to call "organizational transformation." By that I mean the transition "from pyramid to peach," "from centralization to decentralization," "from top-down management to outside-in leadership." I have written entire books and papers filled with the stories of the Toyotas of this world. I have explained their cases and described their unusually smart practices, their principles and discoveries on the way to transformation. I have documented, analyzed and put into context their unique characteristics. Many other authors and experts have done similar stuff.

Case examples appear to tell the stories of galaxies, far far away. But of course they don´t.

However: I cannot honestly claim that these highly impressive case stories have "worked" for my audiences or clients, as much as I would have hoped. Sure, people feel somewhat "inspired" and "motivated" when hearing about the amazing things that happen at Valve, Zappos, Netflix, Morning-Star, Favi or DaVita. When people learn that management tools or practices they consider vital or inevitable simply do not exist within those pioneering organizations, they are in shock and awe. At least for a few moments.

At some point, however, I started asking myself why these wonderful firms have not succeeded in persuading others to follow their example. Why has almost nobody dared to follow in their footsteps? The following anecdote about Ricardo Semler, owner and chief visionary of the trail-blazing "democratic" Brazilian company Semco may illustrate the problem: A few years ago, after two international bestselling books and some 20 years of traveling the international "speaker´s circuit," Semler got so frustrated that nobody was following his company´s example (apart from a small Indian firm), that he took every copy of his books he had at his home, including all translations, into the garden – and set them ablaze!

To be sure: everyone is amazed by these exceptional organizations. They are WOW!, right? But that another company follows their lead seems to be a different matter, entirely. That doesn't happen very often, if at all. It is no coincidence that we are constantly calling these firms "outliers," "radicals," "ground-breaking," "extraordinary," or "exotic." We remind ourselves that they are somehow not from this world. They stake out land that appears unknown and foreign to us. "That would never work for us here," we say. "We're just not ready for that." Or "I could never swing that with my team" and "We went to visit them and had a look; it sure was fascinating, but their approach is just not right for us." How often have I heard those kinds of comments. The most horrific quote of all being: "It's a long, long road to really get there."

For a long time, this seemed to be a contradiction to me. On the one hand, the world of the pioneers really exists – like some continent of copious vegetation. In most people's perception, however, there seems to be no way of entering that secret garden. That land of milk and honey remains out of reach, and foreign, too. In the meanwhile, pioneers like Toyota, Gore, Sweden's Handelsbanken or Germany's dm-drogerie markt keep telling us that there is, really, nothing magic about what they are doing!

Maybe we cannot learn from pioneers like Semco or Toyota because the good example is not the point!

And then it hit me. The trouble with embracing the examples of Semco, Toyota and other pioneers like them may have nothing to do with the pioneering organizations themselves. Nor with what other people think about them – those "other people" being the majority of bosses, managers, company owners and employees. Managers neither lack the courage to transform, nor are they likely

21

to be all scared about the losing control, or the unknown. Maybe, I thought, maybe we cannot learn from pioneers like Semco or Toyota because the good example is not the point!

What I mean is this: When talking about organizational leadership, even the best examples just don't help! At least not as long as one, almost magic ingredient for change, or transformation, is missing. And that magic ingredient is our image of human nature, the way we think about people around us, and what drives them. The key is

---

THE IMAGES OF HUMAN NATURE WE HOLD McGregor´s crucial insight

THEORY X	THEORY Y
ATTITUDE	
People dislike work, find it boring, and will avoid it if they can	People need to work and want to take an interest in it. Under right conditions, they enjoy it
LEADERSHIP	
People must be forced or bribed to make the right effort	People will direct themselves towards a target that they accept
RESPONSIBILITY	
People would rather be directed than accept responsibility (which they avoid)	People will, under the right conditions, seek and accept responsibility
MOTIVATION	
People are motivated mainly by money and fears about their job security	Under the right conditions, people are motivated by the desire to fulfill their own potential
CREATIVITY	
Most people have little creativity – except when it comes to getting around rules	Creativity and ingenuity are widely distributed and grossly underused by organizations

---

not the trust we place in other people, but whether we trust them to be self-motivated, driven by the need for self-fulfillment, and capable of self-organizing within boundaries and team settings. One of my heroes, organizational scientist Douglas McGregor was the first to figure out the power of that crippling, and misleading image of human nature that we hold in our heads and hearts about other people, around 60 years ago. McGregor then coined it "Theory X." The puzzling truth is, that after all this time, the mistaken idea of Theory X thinking still firmly remains part of our belief systems. Theory X works against our best interest, in keeping our organizations stuck in command-and-control mode, driven by top-down, tayloristic management.

BEYOND BLAMING:
APPROACHING SYSTEMS DEVELOPMENT WITH CONSISTENCY

There is great risk in good examples. What we should have learned from McGregor and from his denouncement of the Theory X prejudice, is that neither managers nor employees are the problem when it comes to organizational change and transformation. The problem is our thinking, really. It is our flawed assumption about what makes other people tick, about how the physics of motivation, leadership and change work. Theory X makes us believe that "first our people have to change, and then we can change the system." That is precisely upside-down. The habit of mistrust that is Theory X feeds from our observing other people´s behavior within given contexts. As long as we operate in command-and-control mode, people will usually show obedient, dependent, or even idiotic behavior.

Only when we change the system away from command-and-control, can people develop intelligently aligned behavior patterns, such as those associated with self-organization, empowerment and entrepreneurial responsibility. The problem is that each of us individual keeps thinking: "Yeah, yeah, I got that, things could be way better. But my peers, colleagues and bosses obviously haven't gotten it at all – just look at how they behave! Until they change, we cannot change anything!" Until we overcome this pattern of thinking, which I call the "individual-smarts-collective-stupidity trap," the world of alternative, superior org models and transformation will remain a distant dream of a better future.

In the meanwhile, ironically, it is possible that the examples of pioneers of better org models may even hinder organizational progress and transformation elsewhere. "Look, what happened at Semco and Toyota was possible only because they were already prepared to make it work! Because they had a different kind of human material there that made it all possible. We cannot do that here – our people are not prepared the way they were!" And so the good example becomes a barrier to change.

There is no bridge to the promised land of better, bolder, more agile and contemporary organizational leadership. No one will ever build a bridge there. And nobody really needs that kind of bridge at all. Because we can all beam ourselves there. Our organizations can be flipped into that land of milk and honey, within the twinkling of an eye, as soon as we all stop thinking about other people as "Xers." We do not need more examples for this, we need to correct our thinking. As for Semco, Toyota and the likes: Their example remains noteworthy and potentially inspiring for all of us. Their wonderful stories and practices will remain impossible to emulate, however – as long as we keep carrying around fundamentally screwed-up notions about other people´s human nature.

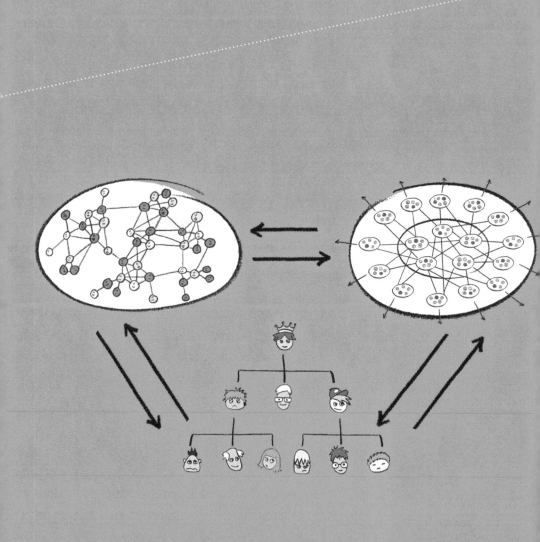

ORGPHYSICS. THE 3 FACES OF EVERY COMPANY: HOW A TRIAD OF STRUCTURES ALLOWS COMPANIES TO ABSORB COMPLEXITY

Since the rise of the corporation at the dawn of the industrial age, much has been said and written about leadership, power, and structure in organizations. Some in the field of organizational research believe that developing a coherent theory of leadership is an illusive, even utopian, undertaking. Most practitioners, on the other side, do not seem to care much about theory at all. Consequently, two sets of beliefs tend to be constantly repeated in our field: On one hand, the tale of heroic leaders and their followers, combined with calls for hierarchical control. On the other hand, the story of the coming end of hierarchy, and future elimination of power within organizations.

Both sides are wrong.

A new, practical theory of leadership, organizational power and structure has emerged. It is ending one of the biggest misunderstandings in organizational science: The notion that organizations can be described through a single structure, a structure that has, since the glory days of the railway corporation in the middle of the 19th century, been usually depicted in the shape of org charts, pyramids and triangles.

While it is clear to most practitioners today that org charts, or connected boxes, cannot even remotely describe organizational complexity and reality, theory and organization development have not advanced much from the original metaphor of organizations as top-down pyramids, lines structures, silos and stand-alone func-

Formal Structure is where you nominated a CEO, and an audit committee. Where you do the bookkeeping and the external reporting. Where you set up contracts of all kinds. This is what this structure is essentially about.

tions. Just a few years back, John P. Kotter started to promote a slightly advanced notion of organizational structure: That of a "dual operating system," of two intertwined structures that could together explain organizational life. The first structure "formal," the other one, described by Kotter in somewhat more fuzzy and generic terms, geared towards the "social" and the interaction. Performance would arise from the interdependence of these structures. The secret was to "build" the second of those two structures.

This is also a misunderstanding. Organizations do not have two faces, but rather three. All of them. And naturally. What John Kotter was missing is how actual work is happening, and what the structural laws behind work and performance are. His way of describing complex social systems as having "operating systems," as in a lifeless machine, is also entirely inappropriate in the context of living systems. The metaphor is simply too simplistic.

The new, emerging theory of organizations is this: Every organization has three kinds of power, three forms of leadership and three

FORMAL STRUCTURE   Power: Hierarchy, or power of position

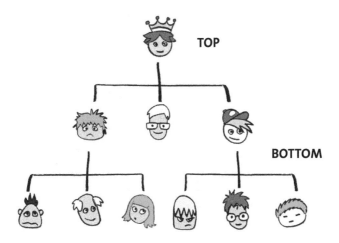

TOP

BOTTOM

structures. This is not a menu. There is no decision to make about having all three structures, or not. None of the three structures is optional, or nice to have. They are part of organizational physics — universal laws that apply to every organization, large or small, old or new, for profit or social.

STRUCTURE NO 1
"FORMAL STRUCTURE" — REALM OF HIERARCHY

The first structure and type of organizational power to turn to is the one we are most familiar with. The most widely understood concept of power in organization is that of hierarchy, which resides within Formal Structure. As a structure, it is neither networked, nor complex, but it is necessary. Its versatility is usually over-estimated, and has been so, since the industrial age.

Formal Structure is capable of producing one important thing: Compliance with regulations. No less, no more. Because Formal Structure is the domain in which compliance is produced, every organization, large or small, old or young, has one.

Formal Structure and hierarchy: Over-estimated and over-emphasized in most organizations. It is this excessive reliance on hierarchy that is the key source of suffering in the world of work today.

But Formal Structure is dramatically over-emphasized in most companies: We make way too much of it, even though many of us suspect that too much use of formal power by managers, or too much emphasis on hierarchy, has serious downsides: As only one of three sources of power within any organization, hierarchy must not be over-emphasized, or the other two will push back, or kick into a dysfunctional mode. The epic struggle between Formal Structure and the other two structures that make up OrgPhysics is one of the key sources of reduced organizational effectiveness, diminished complexity-robustness, and lack of innovation we find today in most companies. Problem is: Most managers, or in fact most working people, are blinded to the other two structures we are about to discover.

STRUCTURE NO 2
"INFORMAL STRUCTURE" — REALM OF INFLUENCE

Informal Structure: Very alive and dynamic. Often taboo. Very powerful. Impossible to accurately pin down or map.

Informal Structure became more popularly known and talked about with the rise of social networks. But it has long been a well-known phenomenon in social sciences. Informal Structure can be thought of as "clouds" of interconnected individuals, with varying numbers of links to others — placing individuals either in central or more peripheral positions in the cloud. Informal Structure is networked. It is neither good, nor bad. Informal Structure is. Think of water cooler and corridor talk,

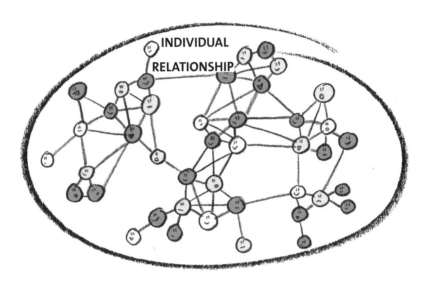

gossip, conspiracy, bullying. But also of solidarity. There is power in the informal. We call this power Influence.

Formal Structure and Informal Structure can be enablers of value creation, and lubricants of work. But they cannot produce performance, success, competitiveness, or value themselves.

An individual´s "sphere of influence" within Informal Structure is not to be confused with the "span of control" that a manager might have in Formal Structure. The nature of the informal is altogether different.

It should be mentioned here that the two structures, and two powers we have looked at so far, are interdependent. So if a CEO mentions that he or she intends to hire a large consulting firm for a "restructuring exercise," this CEO is intervening in both structures: Formal and informal. Both structures will duly react: In Formal Structure, managers will immediately take action to secure their turfs. But part of the reaction is likely to happen within Informal Structure: politics, coalition-building, intrigue — these are phenomena arising from Informal Structure. They can be incredibly powerful, capable of wrecking even the most well-planned change initiative. This is especially true when these efforts are executed by consultants and managers whose repertoire almost exclusively covers interventions suited for Formal Structure.

One of the few large companies that developed mastery in positively acting on and engaging with its Informal Structure is Google. If you want to learn how to carefully curate the informal, learn from them. What have you done lately to irritate your organization´s Informal Structure, constructively?

"VALUE CREATION STRUCTURE" — REALM OF REPUTATION

While Formal Structure is the domain of positions, Value Creation Structure is the domain of work roles. Of which every member of an organization has not one, but many.

This is where OrgPhysics gets most interesting, and most paradigm-shattering. This is the least understood of the three structures of any organization. Ironically, it is also the one structure in which actual work can get done. It is here where the key to a much-improved understanding of organizational effectiveness lies. The only structure from which performance and success can arise. Neither success nor performance can be produced in Formal Structure or Informal Structure, because these are just carriers of the compliance dimension, on one hand, and of the social dimensions of the organization on the other. For actual work or value creation, all organizations possess a third structure: Value Creation Structure.

From this structure arises a particular third kind of power. We call this power Reputation. You have seen power of those with mas-

32

VALUE CREATION STRUCTURE   Power: Reputation, or power of those with mastery

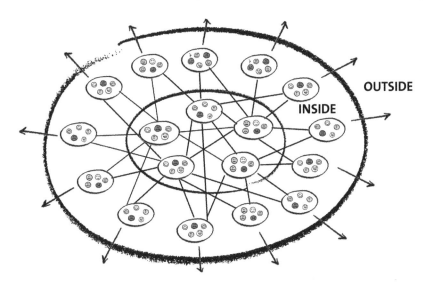

tery, or Reputation, happening. It is when people who have a work problem which they cannot solve on their own, turn to someone else, asking: "Who knows about this?" or "Who is the expert on this particular matter who I can ask about it?" They are looking for mastery, and they can find it by hooking up to the network of power that is Value Creation Structure.

Value Creation Structure is inevitably networked, but in a different way than Informal Structure. All value creation flows from the inside-out: from center, to periphery, to market (for more on this crucial distinction read the *Organize for Complexity* white paper, or book). Value Creation Structures can be mapped as networks of cells, which contain functionally integrated teams, and which are interrelated by value flow, pay, and communication relationships. In this structure, any cell either creates value for other network

It is Value Creation Structure that should come first— not Formal Structure. Only by putting Value Creation first can organizations find balance. Achieve great leaderships. Become aligned with OrgPhysics as they are. cells (in case of the center) or for the outside market (in case of the periphery). Cells, or teams, are supposed to respond to market pull — not hierarchy. It is cells, or teams that create value in their interrelations "with-each-other-for-each-other" — not individuals. Value Creation Structure and its workings make it clear that individual performance, or individual value creation, actually does not exist in organizations. Sadly, Value Creation Structure is rarely well-understood, or consciously curated by organizations. Most of the time it is not even being worked upon systematically — with a few notable exceptions.

One large company that has developed true mastery in empowering and leading through its Value Creation Structure, by turning it into its dominant structure, is Toyota. By putting Value Creation Structure first, Toyota is capable of leveraging the power of all three structures. Here, you can learn a lot about intelligent curation of value creation, through empowerment of teams in the periphery — not through steering by individuals at the top.

EVERY ORGANIZATION
KNOWS THREE KINDS OF LEADERSHIP. NOT JUST ONE

Within the three structures of organizations, three kinds of leadership reside. All important, but dramatically out of balance in most organizations we know:

1. COMPLIANCE LEADERSHIP —
    emerging from Formal Structure.

2. SOCIAL LEADERSHIP —
    emerging from Informal Structure.

THE THREE STRUCTURES Let self-steering, functionally integrated teams compete – not individuals!

INFORMAL STRUCTURE
Social/relationship power = Influence

VALUE CREATION STRUCTURE
Power of those with mastery = Reputation

FORMAL STRUCTURE
Power of position = Hierarchy

3. VALUE CREATION LEADERSHIP —
    emerging from Value Creation Structure.

Following this thought, there is not "leadership." But "leaderships." Just like the three structures they emerge from, these types of leadership are interdependent and complex, not independent or linear. In the presence of too much hierarchy, or formal power, the other two kinds of leadership are actually quite impossible to happen: Social density and connection will deteriorate. Members of the organization will find it harder to get the work done, while they game Formal Structure and its complicated mechanics of steering and control. Organizational energy is wasted on bureaucracy

(Formal Structure), and self-defense against command-and-control from the top, carried out within Informal Structure.

MCGREGOR WAS RIGHT ALL ALONG,
BUT WE FIND HIS MESSAGE INCREDIBLY HARD TO SWALLOW

This is what Douglas McGregor said about structure, power and leadership, in his book *The Human Side of Enterprise*, published in 1960: *"It is probable that one day we shall begin to draw organization charts as a series of linked groups rather than as a hierarchical structure of individual "reporting" relationships."* He was right all along. We have, however, only just started with what McGregor predicted sixty years ago. A new, robust theory of organizational leadership of the kind McGregor theorized about can finally explain organizational complexity, and the complex phenomena of power and leadership within organizations.

A little over 100 years after Frederick W. Taylor´s pioneering, and often misinterpreted, work on management science, we may finally end the quackery around organizational structure, power and leadership. We can employ practical theory that reaches well beyond hierarchy, and that helps us unlock the powers within Value Creation Structure and Informal Structure. These insights about OrgPhysics have long been available to a few outstanding companies, but they have been widely ignored by the wider business community, including academia. By opening our eyes to the true nature of organizational structures, we can greatly, and quite naturally, improve the world of work.

Remember: Every organization has three structures, not one. Ignore them at your own peril.

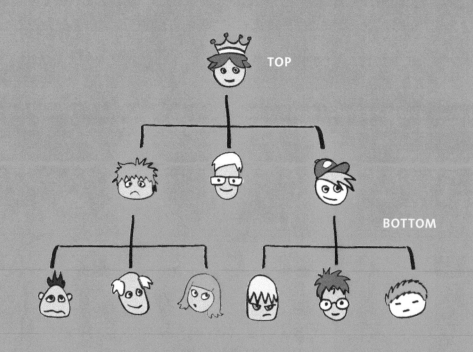

FLAT HIERARCHIES: THEY ARE JUST ANOTHER STEP IN THE WRONG DIRECTION

Most managers and business leaders aim to make their organizations flatter. They try to reduce middle management, to slim the amount of hierarchical layers, or they scrap internal bureaucracy in order to achieve more efficiency, more effectiveness, and more enterprise agility. The problem with this is simple, but important: Organizations should actually not be flat, but decentralized. Why? Because flat means continuing to bark up the wrong tree. In flat, the steering remains from the top.

You cannot want that.

Hierarchical steering in organizations was once a pretty good idea. That was during the industrial age. Since this era ended in the 1970s or so, the ability of markets to surprise us has increased significantly: Value creation in the knowledge age is more dynamic and more prone to surprise than it was in the indus-

Organizations outsourced the steering to markets around forty years ago. trial age. The importance of services, customization, individualized production, uncertainty and highly competitive markets has risen dramatically. That means: in every organization, the outside has to be in charge, top-down has turned into a trap.

As complexity and dynamics reign the markets, confronting organizations with market-pull and ever-more surprise, any kind of centralized counter-push from "above" in the form of command and control ceases to function properly. Steering collapses. If one continues to allow steering from above (or from the inside-out,

VALUE CREATION FROM THE INSIDE-OUT AND TOWARDS THE MARKET:
A key principle for any kind of organization

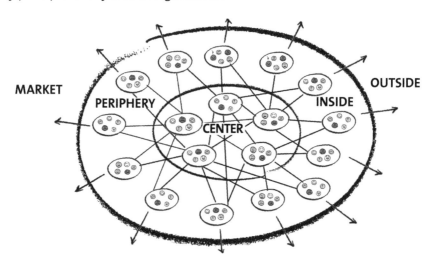

as we will see), then this inevitably leads to "mis-leading", and to hindering or crippling value creation.

THERE IS A BIG DIFFERENCE
BETWEEN MERE DELEGATION, AND DECENTRALIZATION

Flat hierarchies are thus not a solution at all, but actually the continuation, or perpetuation of a management tradition that has long since turned into a mistake. If an organization today does not turn towards the outside market, consistently, but remains in the mode of vertical steering, then middle management will always grow back. The same goes for bureaucratic steering rituals – such as target negotiation, micro-management, budgeting, planning processes, allocations, cost management, and excessive rules and policies.

Those who talk of layers of resistance in the middle have not yet understood the problem.

It is only in the mode of "decentralized" that the reason for having a middle management and centralized steering disappears entirely. Here, self-organization and leadership from the outside-in becomes possible. Once we accept the notion that markets can steer organizations, as long as they possess decentralized autonomy and decision-making, we recognize that internal steering is dispensable. Hierarchy becomes recognized as a trivial phenomenon. Value creation towards the market, from center to periphery to customer can become the dominant principle. Value creation can flow – unhindered by steering.

It is only in _decentralized_ mode that any reason for having a middle management disappears entirely.

So you better quit trying to make your company "flatter." In complexity, an organization must be federative – not flat. When outside markets rule, then it is the part of the organization that we call the periphery that earns the money. It is the periphery

41

DECENTRALIZATION AS DEVOLUTION OF AUTONOMY
and decision-making power to the periphery

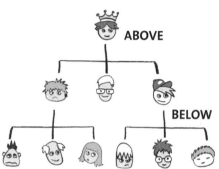

INDUSTRIAL AGE
divided, individualizing work the
people top-down, managed
in parallel, next to each other

KNOWLEDGE AGE
integrated, team-based work the work,
work the system outside-in, led
with-each-other-for-each-other

that learns from the market the easiest; that can best adapt to
and respond to markets — quickly and intelligently. In complexity,
the center loses its information monopoly, its competence advantage: it can hardly issue any meaningful commands any more.
The coupling between periphery and center must consequently
be designed in a way that enables the organization to absorb and
process market dynamics. For that, the periphery must steer the
center through market-like mechanisms and own the monetary
resources. Not the other way around. (But hey, the periphery earns
the money anyways, right?)

Decentralization works according to laws different than those of
hierarchy. Where the principle of decentralization is applied consis-

tently, then autonomy and decision-making power are increasingly given back to teams in the periphery. Such a process of "devolution of autonomy" from the center to the periphery can go on, and on, and on for decades.

Decentralization never ends.

CHANGE-AS-FLIPPING: CHANGE IS MORE LIKE ADDING MILK TO COFFEE

Change is not a journey. Never has been. Trouble is: Change agents around the world have been imagining change as projects, programs, planned exercises to be "kicked off" and "implemented." We have interpreted change as difficult ventures, endlessly long hikes, and exhaustive trips. No more: Here are 5 key insights into the true nature of change, and into how to create profound, transformational change, effortlessly and fast. Sounds impossible? Then check out these concepts for a more constructive and robust alternative to change management, or planned change, as you know it.

The most widely used metaphors for change are related to that of a journey from the current state (often labeled 'status quo') to the desired state (a.k.a. 'vision'). The desired state, in this metaphor, is seen as a place out there in the future. Or as a north star – never quite to be reached. We have been lead to believe that change-as-a-journey has to be long and strenuous, that it is hard and danger-ous. Consequently, armed with delusional road maps, project plans, or blueprints, we embark on what we imagine will be a long and difficult journey. We start to foresee all sorts of obstacles – that don't actually exist, as we will see later in this article. But we find ourselves believing the milestones we invented are real, and get anxious when they don't appear on the horizon.

This approach misrepresents change as a "controllable process" composed of a sequence of discrete stages, phases or steps; and it deludes us into thinking we have to make a map for getting from the current state of affairs to the desired state. This approach trivializes change. We call this approach "Planned Change". This is what we commonly think change management is all about: plan-ning and controlling the change journey. The journey metaphor tricks us into ignoring the possibility that the desired change might be accomplished quickly, with little effort, right now, with existing resources and with mini-mal disruption. The metaphor itself makes change hard.

Profound transformation never takes more than two years – inde-pendent if it´s about an organization with 20 people, or 200.000.

Now, spill a tiny bit of milk into coffee, and with this tiny nudge a new pattern is instantly being created. It's altogether different from the original one, pure coffee, and the change is permanent. There is no way of returning to the first pattern. This is much more similar to what change actually is than calling change a journey.

Change is like adding milk to coffee.

This is a more helpful metaphor than the widespread notion of seeing change as a "journey from here to there." It means to see change as something of a flip from Now (the current state) to New (the desired state). What is important: Both Now and New are in the present, not in the future. The New can be produced right here, right now. Profound change, different than problem solving, requires a sequence of flips. Or many flips. Maybe a few hundred, maybe a few thousand. But still, every flip will have its own, immediate impact. Create a changed reality.

Profound change means sequenced flipping of the system from Now to New – right here, right now. A thousand times or more.

INSIGHT 2.
THERE IS NO SUCH THING AS RESISTANCE TO CHANGE –
ONLY SMART RESPONSE TO DUMB METHOD

The man who invented Resistance in Change is Kurt Lewin, one of my heroes. Lewin, the brilliant founder of social psychology and organizational change as such, introduced the term resistance as a systems concept: as a force affecting managers and employees equally. Unfortunately, only the terminology, but not the context, was popularized. We now cast resistance as a psychological, individualized issue, personalizing it as "employees versus managers."

In this mental model, it is always the others. Employees "resist," top management "is not committed." We judge others saying things like: "They have an interest in preserving the status quo." The "They" is very important, of course. The resistance assumption is implicitly arrogant. As long as we accept this mental model, it confuses our understanding of change dynamics. It perpetuates the status quo of command-and-control organization. It´s better to let go of the term and embrace more helpful mental models for change. So let´s give it a try:

People don´t resist change.

Can you say that to yourself, in your head? Now that is a start. But what is behind the behavior, then, that we are observing all the time, in change efforts, if it is not resistance to change? Take a step back and you will see that people act consciously and intelligently (overall), to other things than the change itself. They may resist loss of status and power – which is quite intelligent. They may resist injustice, stupidity and being changed. Which is also intelligent. The change may also cause need for new learning that is not properly addressed. And these are the things that we have to deal with in change: power structures, status, injustice, consequence, our own stupidity, top-down command-and-control, and learning.

The more resistance to change you observe, the more likely it is that your methods suck.

Instead of watching out for the possibility of resistance, we should watch out for the common mistakes in creating intentional change and deal with the perfectly natural reactions to (our) poor interventions. Without resorting to blame.

Let me be clear: The notion that people resist change is not held up by social sciences. It is actually completely opposed to our scientific knowledge about human capability to change (Alan Deutschman wrote a wonderful, summarizing book about this, called *Change or Die*). It is a fairy-tale that people resist change. There are symptoms of struggle with adaption and the new that should not be confused with resistance to the change itself. Once you start with that kind of projection, the trouble really starts. We generally tend to have a hard time imagining future possibilities, though. This is why any change effort will have to deal with the need for imagination, or visioning.

INSIGHT 3.

THE PROBLEM IS IN THE SYSTEM –
ALMOST ALWAYS

If resistance does not come from people, then where does it reside? Resistance is much more likely to be found elsewhere. Edwards W. Deming said: "94% of the problems in business are system-driven and only 6% are people-driven." Which means: If the problem is in the system, almost always, then change should mostly be about working the system.

Removing obstacles in the system to promote profound change is clearly easier than introducing entirely new features, rituals or memes within a system. This is what makes the concept of Organizational Hygiene such a compelling idea (see page 144). Whether you are removing something, or introducing something new while flipping from Now to New: producing change effectively in organizations requires specific, targeted action on the system – not blaming. This means: if the anticipated change will result in the loss of status by some employees, then we must develop strategies for dealing with the loss of status. Likewise, if the change will result in the loss of jobs, that issue must be dealt with. If the change will result in the need for new learning, then let's take care of that. If the change will come at an emotional cost, then there should be a space for emotions and mourning. Labeling these difficult, real-life problems as resistance to change only impedes the process. Resistance becomes a self-fulfilling prophecy. Put differently:

Change done well does not produce losers.
Only consequences.

Power interests are also very real and often ignored by change "agents." They should not. John Kotter stated that individual resistance out of self-interest exists, but that it is "rare." More often, he said, the obstacle is in the organization's structure or in a "performance appraisal system [that] makes people choose between the new vision and their own self-interest." In other words:

What we interpret as resistance to change
is an intelligent response to inconsistencies
between the organizational model
and the desired state.

Change, in this sense, is successive re-negotiation of the organizational model – not revolution! Kotter´s NoNo has good reasons to oppose the change – reasons that are probably triggered by the current system, not the individual´s twisted psyche. Again: What we observe should ultimately be coined lack of consequence, not resistance to change.

Which all leads us back to the conclusion: In change-as-constant-flipping, we must work the system with the people, instead of working the people within the system. Diverting from this path leads to blaming, and almost inevitable to self-induced failure of our change efforts.

INSIGHT 4.
ORGANIZATIONAL CHANGE IS SOCIALLY DENSE -
THE TECHNICAL SIDE IS (ALMOST) TRIVIAL

The idea of Emergent Change, or continuous flipping from Now to New acknowledges that change happens within a complex pattern that cannot be predicted or controlled – only observed. One of the first to describe this kind of thinking on change coherently was

Kotter. His approach outlines profound change as a dense, social movement: The collective, emergent side of change, so to say. The element that was still be missing from Kotter´s change approach is the individual side of change – the need for individual adaptation that members of an organization have to undergo to flip or when flipping. Adding the individual side of org change to the collective side, one starts perceiving change as two-dimensional. We call this the Double-Helix nature of change.

Method must always be appropriately complex, and social.

Many change agents are enamored with their method of choice. Many of us like to believe that this method or tool is wonderful, effective and impactful. Change as flipping, however, is based on the assumption that

Relationship is everything,
method is secondary.

There are many decent or effective methods, but what really matters is creating different relationships within the system, and relationships of higher quality. Many methods can help doing that. In fact, the more complex the problem is, the more complex, or social, the method must be. Nothing is worse than crystallized method – or "dead" method, applied to living problems. We will explore this aspect of change and complexity-robust methods in other articles of this book.

INSIGHT 5.
THERE IS NO SUCH THING AS TRANSFORMATION -
INSTEAD, EVERYTHING IS AN INTERVENTION

I am guilty. I am guilty of talking about transformation myself. A lot. And I liked it! I liked to say things like: *Organizations should transform from the organizational model of the industrial age ("Alpha") to a contemporary, complexity-robust one ("Beta").* I keep saying that kind of thing, occasionally, even though I know the term transformation is neither helpful, nor accurate. Sometimes I just can´t help it!

The truth is probably closer to: There is no transformation. Because:

> *Constant flipping is the only thing*
> *there is in change.*

This is consistent with the old adage "Everything is an intervention." Which is one of the most beautiful things that has ever been said about change (which probably is a rather misleading term, as well). That everything is an intervention does not mean, of course, that every intervention is good in itself. It just means that everything, really everything, influences, or potentially flips an organization.

Organizations are being flipped all the time. Question is: Is the flipping done with intent, or is it arbitrary? Do the flips foster self-organization, decentralization and team autonomy?

Instead of change management, we should practice the craft of change as exercising constructive irritation – as we like to say in systems theory. According to systems theory (outlined by authors such as Niklas Luhmann), the only thing you can do is to irritate a system. Then observe the consequences and ripple effects. Then irritate again. Then observe. And so on. Any irritation can flip the system into the New state. If you are lucky and if the irritation was smart enough, the state is a form of desired state.

In any case: irritate again. This is never supposed to be over. Change is not a journey, remember? Welcome to the world of, well: Eternal flipping.

YOUR COMPANY
HAS EXACTLY
THE CULTURE
IT DESERVES

Culture is part of an organization's memory. Another way
to put this: Your company´s culture is like a shadow! You can observe it. You may find it more or less to your liking. But culture, or
that shadow, does not care. You cannot change the shadow —
even though it constantly moves, shifts, and changes.

One might say: Culture is read-only.

Why should this matter to managers, entrepreneurs, executive boards, and to people in organizations, overall? Because in our conversations around culture, we unfailingly talk about the wrong things. We talk about the "risk culture" of our companies. About cost culture, or better, the lack thereof. Sometimes we talk about cultures of corruption and waste; about lacking quality consciousness; about (a lack of) innovation culture; we ask, is our culture "mature enough" for this tool, for that change? *"Can we do this, given our culture?" "We are now developing our culture further!"* All that amounts to nothing more than shadow-boxing. The truth is: You cannot work on your organization´s culture. What you can do, and should do, is work your organization, instead.

Culture does not bind us, it does not ordain anything. Culture only tells us what is considered "normal" today and what is not. *"This thing is common and a part of our organization's style – that is not."* In this way, culture is conservative by nature: you cannot ask culture if it would like to be different. Its culture simply trails the organization. Culture is completely and cruelly indifferent: It not only mirrors the official, or the desired state of an organization, but also the backstage and the dark corners. If we were sloppy or inconsequential a few years or some months ago; if we shirked an unpleasant decision: It ends up showing up in the culture. In that sense, culture is merciless.

At one bank where I consulted, the saying went that branch employees were lacking commitment and entrepreneurial spirit. As this was a rather mature institution that had gone through the occasional painful merger, those behavioral patterns observed in the branches was tagged as a classic "culture problem."

Let's ignore for the moment that statements referring to "the others" – in this case the branches – usually amount to no more than blaming. Over time, we found out that branch employees at the bank neither lacked commitment, consciousness and passion, nor entrepreneurial spirit at all. There sure were scars from past mergers and crises, but those appeared to play a much smaller role than what prejudice at headquarters suggested. What we learned, instead: As a branch employee, acting upon one´s entrepreneurial consciousness had, over time, become systemically impossible. Just as citizens of the GDR (former East Germany) would not have had a picnic in the Berlin Wall´s "death zone."

CULTURE DOES NEITHER BLOCK NOR ENABLE CHANGE.
IT IS A TOOL THAT YOU MAY USE FOR WORKING THE SYSTEM

If neither hearts nor minds of branch employees were the barriers to performance in this bank – what were the actual barriers? The usual, one might say. Nothing of what follows will surprise you. Here is just a small selection of toxic artifacts we encountered within that company´s systems: Rules and regulations galore – many of them nonsensical. Quotas, price lists, incentive systems, bonuses and growth-targets, budgets, performance indicators, an uninterrupted meeting circus, hierarchical pressure, constant campaign pressure, top-down decisions, bans, instructions, any internal (and external) bureaucracy, marketing budgets, cost control, travel cost regulations, forms, central divisions ("marketing," "HR," "finance"), other divisions, departmental limits, steering by bosses and the bosses of bosses.

Culture is capable of making lunacy invisible and of making the lunatic appear logical.

Too bad we got so used to all these artifacts that we consider them "normal," right? Take note: *That* is the power of culture. It makes the crazy seem normal and much of the normal seems crazy. It assimilates its members – without remorse. Culture is capable of making lunacy invisible and making the lunatic appear logical. That's also the reason why employee surveys and culture surveys are a complete waste of time and money. Those tools are like asking the blind about things they cannot see. Sensible answers are unlikely – effective conclusions impossible.

The absorbing power of culture in turn means that "new" colleagues are a valuable resource for anyone who really wants a "better" culture and to establish deep organizational change. New colleagues, and more precisely those who joined less than three or six months ago, are still capable of seeing the beauty and madness before becoming blind to it. To them, the organization is still fresh and "not normal" (yet) – until they are assimilated by the culture, too, within just a few months time.

Culture as a tool for change works somewhat like the *camera obscura*. The new member of an organization, or mere strangers, can look through it and grasp the essence of the organization. Observing culture in this way will produce pictures that may sometimes appear upside-down, that may look funny or seem blurred. At least until the brain adapts to the view. But finding a way to observe a culture is not going to change anything by itself. You also have to act.

Because:

YOUR COMPANY HAS EXACTLY
THE CULTURE IT DESERVES

If you do not like your company´s culture, you have to work the organization´s system. Culture does not care what you think of it – or what you wish for. Work the organization itself, preferably together with others, instead of trying to beat the shadow.

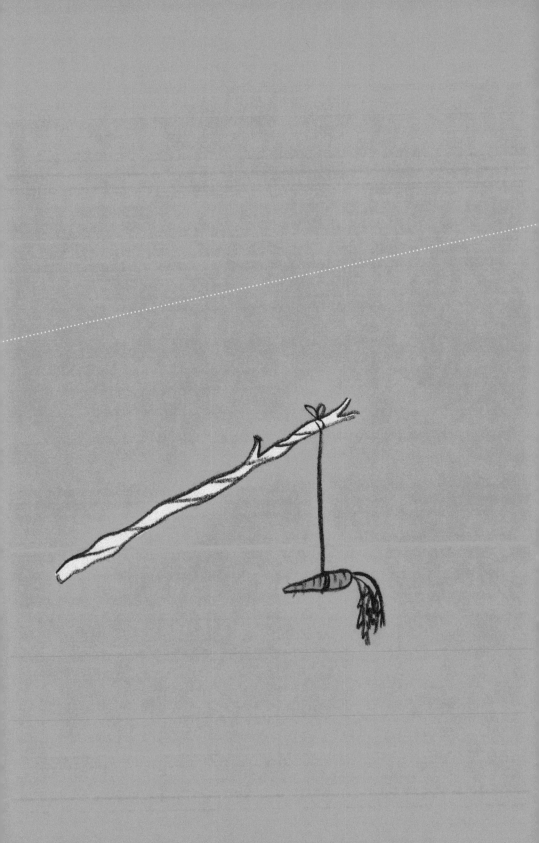

ABOLISH BONUSES! THERE IS NO WAY AROUND THAT

The days of the sophisticated systems of variable compensation are over.

Once upon a time, there was a bank that had many, many employees. It was an ambitious bank, one that held itself in high regard. Also, it thought of itself as beautiful and very, very smart, deserving more success than any other bank in the realm. This bank once heard the story of a stupid donkey and its rider who dangled a carrot in front of the donkey. The donkey would follow the eternally unattainable vegetable – very much to the delight of the rider.

Thus the bank conceived the following ruse: Not only would its employees receive a decent salary, it would also additionally motivate them to improve company performance – just like the donkey rider in the story! So one day, the bank started offering its people incentives. Some kind of turnip. And since the bank knew a lot about money and not much about nutrition and vegetables, it used money, instead of carrots. It started calling its turnips "bonuses." And lo and behold – something duly happened.

At this point I guess I can cut the story short – it's all over town already, anyways: bonuses and incentive systems do not actually work with human beings – regardless of how smart and sophisticated their designs are. Incentives neither improve individual performance (if there is such a thing) nor company results. Why? Well, incentive systems have as much in common with performance as intelligence tests have to do with intelligence. That is, nothing at all. Intelligence tests do not measure intelligence, but the ability to solve tests; bonuses do not cause better-performing employees or better company performance, but employees who find ways to get their bonuses. Nothing more. Nothing less. To call bonus systems "pay for performance" or "meritocratic" systems, therefore, is utterly absurd.

> Intelligence tests do not measure intelligence, but the ability to solve tests; bonuses do not cause better performing employees, but that employees find ways to get their bonus.

THE FATAL EFFECTS OF INCENTIVES ON BEHAVIOR
are everywhere

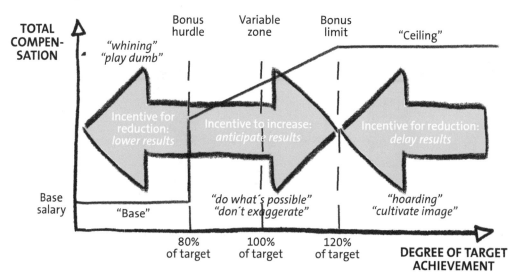

The problem is not that employees are dumb, because exactly the opposite is true. In the 1990s, Harvard professor Michael Jensen illustrated how incentive pay really works: by coupling compensation to goals you introduce "breaks" into the total compensation (see illustration). These breaks prompt incentivized individuals to exploit the system for their individual advantage, to the detriment of the whole system. This happens in every situation possible. In other words: Through incentive systems, people are incentivized to game the system, and to eventually break the system.

Incentives and bonuses are compensation practices from the past. They belong on the garbage heap of history.

The compensation systems we are discussing are not harmless at all. Without the "aggressive," "motivational" pay and bonus culture, the financial crisis of 2008 would never have reached the dimensions it eventually had. Presumably, the crisis would never even have happened: incentives turn incentivized people into donkeys. They put blinders on them and rendered their behaviors apparently insane. Incentives implicitly tell managers and employees: "Reach your goal and you are fine! Do not worry if customers are happy, if you add value to the company, or if laws are broken. Just make the numbers we are giving you."

THE BANKING INDUSTRY MAY BE EXTREME IN ITS USE OF BONUSES BUT IT IS BY NO MEANS AN EXCEPTION

The financial service sector is obviously permeated by the bonus and incentive culture like no other. Here, the variable parts of total salaries are – with some exceptions – high or very high. And the ample use of variable pay has been well established within banks for decades. As a consequence, many bank executives, personnel managers as well as controllers and members of bank's supervisory boards find it hard to imagine how pay systems in their industry might work differently. This does not reduce the urgency to step away from these remuneration practices, however. Quite the opposite: the shortcomings of the financial industry, such as low quality of advice to clients, compliance and ethical violations, or extreme volatility of results and company valuations, are insurmountable without abandoning its current compensation culture.

Swiss bank UBS provides a striking example of how irredeemably broken incentive systems are. Repeatedly, and always with great fanfare, UBS has turned its incentive systems upside-down – most recently in 2012/2013. Yet those efforts always amounted to near-nothing: in the end, they just optimized the wrong thing. Despite assurances to the contrary, fixed targets, performance incentives, stock option programs, and elaborate "allocations" have stayed in place at UBS. It is clear that the near-endless chain of scandals at this bank and others will never stop this way! Bonuses predictably produce internal rat races – which you cannot end by just tweaking incentive systems. You must get rid of incentives once and for all.

But what does an alternative to incentives and to bonuses linked into individual, fixed targets, look like? Incentive-less pay systems, first of all, are much simpler and more cost-effective than the systems currently in place at UBS and so many other firms. The simplest solution of all: Pay people fixed salaries exclusively. To do that, just turn the formerly "variable" part of the salary into the fixed base salary. Total personnel cost will not increase through that change, or "flip." It just officially fixes what previously was supposed to be variable. Another option for designing incentive-less variable pay is to give people a share of team (not: individual!) results or profit, e.g. in the shape of profit sharing or company shares or team result sharing. Always avoid stock options, though: They always create an incentive for manipulation and misrepresentation.

In my views, the problem with manager and employee pay in the finance industry and beyond is not so much one of absolute compensation, or total salaries. Banker´s salaries today are often excessive and at times brazen, for sure. Overly high salaries are a problem the banks themselves and their owners most suffer from. Incentive systems, on the other hand, pose a threat to our societies at large. Such pay systems condition people to turn a blind eye, to abuse society, to make the numbers at all costs: *"Fulfill your quota. Come hell or high water, even if it breaks the company."* This is fatal, consider how financial services have become an indispensable part of our economies. Societies as a whole require reliable and responsible financial services to function.

As long as there are compensation systems tied to revenue, individual targets, plans and forecasts, distrust in the financial industry is justified and will never go away. My point is: People **Managers are** who work in organizations, including managers and **not greedy *per sé.*** bankers, are not overly greedy. But they are made **They are made greedy** overly greedy by today´s performance management **by typical performance** systems. Through so-called "Performance Manage- **management systems.** ment Systems," people are systematically rewarded to be selfish, greedy, non-collaborative and distrustful. Incentives and bonuses are remuneration practices from the past. They belong on the garbage heap of history. The CEOs, the chairmen, the supervisory boards, and shareholders of this world must step up and make the move away from incentive systems happen.

In the long run, every company has exactly the people it deserves. Do your managers, employees, or colleagues behave like donkeys?

BYE-BYE MANAGEMENT BY OBJECTIVES! FROM FIXED TO RELATIVE PERFORMANCE

For decades, organizations of all sizes and from all kinds of industries have curated and perfected management practices such as fixed target setting, target negotiation, planning, budgeting, forecasting, plan-actual variance reporting, incentives-setting, and individual performance appraisal. Now, things are changing: Those practices, usually combined under brands such as Management by Objectives, Merit Pay, or Pay-for-Performance have recently come under fire. If markets and work are becoming ever more dynamic, then how can static, annual rituals remain effective and appropriate to improve or even control performance?

Look at companies large and small, and everywhere in the world, and you will find that performance management practices these days are remarkably alike, almost everywhere. That bundle of management practices was popularized between the 1950s and the 1980s, starting with the idea of Management by Objectives, proposed by Peter Drucker in his 1954 book, and into the late 1970s, when Michael Porter elevated the idea of competitive advantage, or strategy, to a quasi-science. Since then, "fixed performance contracts" have become almost omnipresent and are until this day considered the standard for managing performance, and for controlling businesses and people.

Starting with the Beyond Budgeting movement in the late 1990s, some have started to question the idea of the static performance contract: the philosophy of budgeting and setting fixed targets in advance, and then measuring and judging actual performance against those predefined objectives. Fixed performance contracts, the critics say, are inefficient today, they are counter-productive in times when uncertainty and surprise become the norm, and when value-creation becomes more complex, instead of remaining just complicated.

PERFORMANCE MANAGEMENT: ARE WE RIDING A DEAD HORSE?

The side-effects of "fixed performance contracts" are wide-ranging and dramatic. They range from internal stakeholders gaming performance systems and controls (in reaction to target-setting and bonus compensation), to external stakeholders and CFOs rigging the financial markets (in reaction to earnings guidance and expectation management). In other words: The performance management practices from the past are broken, and we know it. Uncertainty and complexity have long invalidated planning, forecasting, fixed targets, plan-actual reporting (see illustration "How we fool ourselves"), and bonus systems. We have outsourced control to markets a long time ago. But instead of letting go of all practices that assume stable, slow-moving, and indeed dull markets, we have continued to optimize and perfect these practices. We have tried to improve a way of managing that has long been

HOW WE FOOL OURSELVES, USING FIXED PERFORMANCE CONTRACTS:
Example of a financial performance indicator

Fixed, top-down/negotiated targets
Example: Absolute Return in % (here: 15 %)

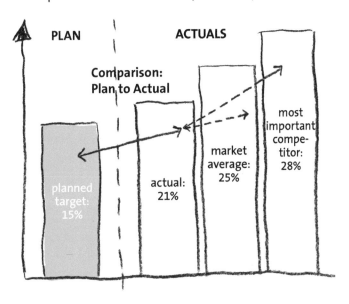

› Interpretation within the plan-actual-comparison: "Plan was outperformed by 6 percentage points" > positive interpretation

› Better ROCE of the market average and the performance of the most important competitor remain unnoticed!

straight jackets, or "dead horses." The very same Peter Drucker once wrote that "90% of what we call management today actually consists of practices that make it hard for people to do their work." Today, the challenge for us is not just to recognize that, and its consequences. It is to get off the dead horse. In dynamic markets and value creation, absolute targets weaken control and create

A BETTER ALTERNATIVE, USING RELATIVE PERFORMANCE CONTRACTS:
Example of a financial performance indicator

Relative, self-adjusting targets
Example: Relative Return in % to market

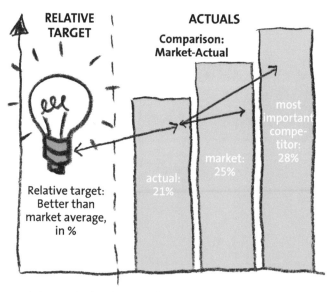

> Interpretation in actual-actual comparison: "Performance was 4 percentage points below competition!" > negative interpretation

> Absolute assumptions at the moment of planning don't matter. Targets always remain updated and relevant!

misleading incentives (see illustration on page 69), while relative measurement enables transparency and adaptive control rooted in self-organization principles (see left).

The good news is that the solution, or the alternative to fixed performance contracts, has been around for quite a while, albeit in a relatively small number of startlingly successful "pioneering" organizations. These alternatives may seem new and counter-intuitive to many companies and managers today who have been used to the notion of controlling through fixed performance contacts. But some larger companies have used relative performance contracts, exclusively, for a few decades. As we learned during the case study research journey of the Beyond Budgeting Round Table that started in 1998, there is a whole world beyond budgeting, beyond fixed targets, incentives and variance reporting. We began labeling this alternative "relative performance contracts" in the early 2000s.

Relative performance contracts are based on the assumption that it is unwise to set fixed targets for managers and teams and then to control their behavior and activities in terms of these targets. The implicit agreement is that management's task is to provide a challenging and open work climate within which employee teams agree to aim for continuous performance improvements: managers and employees must use their knowledge and their own common sense to adapt to changing conditions and environments.

TOWARDS THE EMERGING "RELATIVE" PERFORMANCE CONTRACTS

Under this new performance contract, decisions are not made at the top. Instead, they are distributed, decentralized, and devolved as far out as possible. This type of contract increases, not erodes, mutual trust. Increased transparency and higher expectations

HOW TO "MOVE UP"
from fixed to relative performance contracts

› Transparency & Improvement
› Comparisons between peers
› Comparisons with previous periods
› Dialog and Dissent
› Social and group pressure
› Pay by market value
› Results-sharing

› Fixed, individual targets
› Management by Objectives
› Budgets and Plans
› Performance Appraisal
› Hierarchical Pressure
› Pay by Position or Performance
› Incentives and Bonuses

(compared to competitors or their equivalent) provide a permanent challenge, which has to be mastered by teams. Bad performance, compared to peers, will lead to equally transparent consequences. Responsibility for performance and decision-making are gradually shifted away from individuals at the center of the organization towards teams, or cells in the periphery. Decentralization thus is key to relative performance contracts.

Variations of this kind of relative measurement have been used by a few larger companies for decades. An example: In 1971, after severe internal crisis, Swedish bank Handelsbanken began to

WAYS OF MEASURING
without actual-plan-variances, fixed targets, or plans

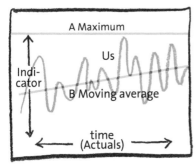

TREND WITH REFERENCES

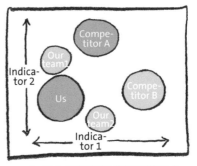

**ACCOUNTS/INDICATORS
VS PREVIOUS PERIODS**

Last month	Same month last year	Same month prev. year	Ø last 12 mnths	Ø 12 prev. mnths

Indicators or groups of accounts

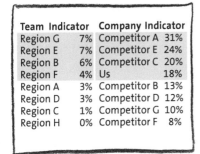

Team Indicator		Company Indicator	
Region G	7%	Competitor A	31%
Region E	7%	Competitor E	24%
Region B	6%	Competitor C	20%
Region F	4%	Us	18%
Region A	3%	Competitor B	13%
Region D	3%	Competitor D	12%
Region C	1%	Competitor G	10%
Region H	0%	Competitor F	8%

**TEAM RANKINGS (LEAGUE TABLES)
INTERNAL/EXTERNAL**

**FLASHLIGHT WITH INTERNAL/
EXTERNAL BENCHMARKS**

Indicator 2 / Indicator 1 / Competitor A / Competitor B / Our team 1 / Our team 2 / Us

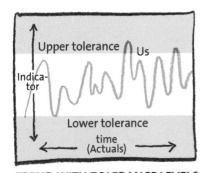

TREND WITH TOLERANCE LEVELS

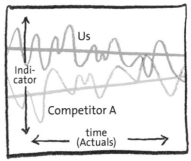

TREND WITH BENCHMARK

73

transform its organizational units into self-managed profit centers with clearly defined customer relationships and highly devolved responsibility for the results. Budgets, fixed targets, quotas, incentives and bonus systems, and indeed also the org chart, and central departments like marketing, product management and risk were abolished. Handelsbanken now has over 10,000 employees and it has consistently been Europe´s most successful bank for more than 42 years, in pretty much any performance indicator you can imagine. This bank´s branch network now consists of more than 700 subsidiaries, legally independent regional banks, and service departments. Autonomy of the bank's branches has been extended continuously since the 1970s. The company's main focus is on branch effectiveness, not on the profitability of individual products.

RELATIVE PERFORMANCE SYSTEMS
FOR A NEW AND MORE COMPLEXITY-ROBUST KIND OF CONTROL

To monitor performance, Handelsbanken developed a compellingly simple control system within which teams work on the basis of relative performance measurement based on "real world," not planned, performance data. Success is no longer measured according to negotiated, planned data, but relative improvement as measured using a limited number of key figures. To do this, the bank as a whole, compares itself with its closest rivals. Similarly, regional banks assess their performance monthly and in comparison with other regions, and branches are compared with other branches. All targets, performance assessments and reporting systems are thus based on internal or external competition and continuous improvement.

This continuous, 3-layer ranking system has proved to be highly self-regulating and has required only minor modifications over the course of decades. It does not require any annual adjustment, nor does it depend on hierarchically integrated planning, or internal negotiation. At the same time, it has dramatically increased internal transparency and responsibility of teams who act as if "the branch is the bank." Employees are driven not by individual targets or group incentives; rather, the system appeals to employees' need to be valued and recognized for their role in helping the organization succeed.

WE KNOW THAT FIXED PERFORMANCE CONTRACTS
DO NOT WORK.
WHAT ARE WE WAITING FOR?

Other larger, successful companies such as Southwest Airlines, Toyota, W.L. Gore, Guardian Industries, Aldi, dm-drogerie markt, or Egon Zehnder International have developed relative performance systems similar to the Handelsbanken approach. There are enough examples of pioneering companies to give us the courage to overcome traditional thinking and ways of dealing with performance. Now that competitive benchmark data is becoming more widely available (to organizations of all kinds and sizes), at much lower cost than ever before, we have ever more reasons to search for new ways to measure and improve performance more effectively: using real, relative data, instead of numbers that were invented.

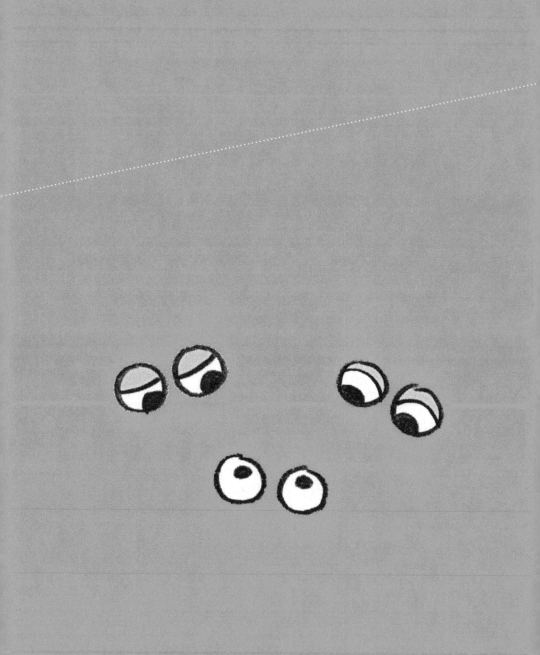

SOCIAL DENSITY: THE KEY TO SELF-ORGANIZATION

Command-and-control (a.k.a. management, the social technology) is "socially loose." Here, pressure is performed from the top-down. Control works just the same way. Quite simply: In this way of operating, it is always the top of the organization that is in charge. Variations of the command-and-control theme include "delegation," "participation," or temporarily tolerating "islands of happiness" within the organization. Each variation offers slightly different rules and patterns - as long as they do not destabilize the whole. Command-and-control has been the standard way of operating organizations for what appears to be forever: We all know precisely how command-and-control works. The problem is a different one, however: Too many of us have long since accepted the notion that other, more effective forms of organization based on self-organization principles (a.k.a. real leadership) are "less likely" to happen, "more difficult," "more chaotic/risky" and/or "less efficient." It is this continuing disbelief in self-organization that starts the trouble: by accepting notions such as the above, our own thinking turns into the biggest barrier to the Necessary Organizational Renaissance.

Self-organization is very different from command-and-control. It is, one might say, about disciplined togetherness. Self-organization is always about "being socially dense, collectively." Once we think about organizations in terms of social density, it becomes clear that self-organization cannot be appropriately described through the metaphors of "top-down," or "bottom-up." If anything, self-organization is about acknowledging outside-in market-pull, which relentlessly applies its forces on any organization today. Then, within an organization, these pull-forces from outside markets must be responded to, constructively, through inside-out value creation.

Self-organization is about disciplined togetherness. About being socially dense, collectively.

In short: Organizations actually neither have heads, nor asses. Instead, they consist of outside-in pull dynamics, as well as inside-out value creation dynamics that materialize between units of value creation, usually referred to as teams. Looking at organizations that way, it is fair to say that they all have in fact outsourced the steering to markets a long, long time ago. Which is why market-driven, socially dense self-organization became way more effective than top-down steering, beginning in the 1970s.

Control, in self-organization, arises from within the team structure. The most important mechanisms of control are a combination of 1) transparency – the capability of everyone, and every team, having access to all information, and potentially looking at it in the same way; and 2) peer pressure, or social pressure. Which is not as bad as it may sound at first! Think of it in terms of self-organization and as the total opposite of top-down tyranny, or George Orwell´s novel 1984. While command-and-control tends to individualize the members of the organization, self-organization always focuses on the team (not the individual) as the smallest unit of performance. And the team is always a social unit.

There are a few pre-conditions, in addition to transparency, that are necessary to enable coherent, team-based social density, even in the largest organizations.

1. FIRSTLY, PEER PRESSURE, IT TURNS OUT, IS ONLY LIKELY TO HAPPEN IF JOINT TEAM PERFORMANCE IS MEASURED, CONTINUOUSLY — as opposed to measuring supposed individual performance through negotiated targets, personal measures or appraisal. This can be achieved by using Relative Targets and performance contracts (see previous essay). And by abolishing all individual targets/measures, and performance appraisal, and bonuses.

2. SECONDLY, YOU NEED SHARED PRINCIPLES (AS OPPOSED TO RULES) which bind team members and the organization as a whole to joint standards of behavior, guarded by everyone. Rules, by contrast, bind people into obedience and followership — something that runs counter to self-organization, of course. This can be achieved by eliminating all rules (such as time controls and travel policies), and by iteratively agreeing on a compact set of highly prominent principles, deployed organization-wide. An example of such a principle: "We will always use our available resources responsibly and frugally." Principles can be socialized through a "Letter to Ourselves" for the organization.

Decentralization and self-organization: They are the two sides of the same coin.

3. THIRDLY, PEER PRESSURE REQUIRES PEOPLE WITH MASTERY TO BE IN CHARGE — as opposed to accentuation of positional, formal power. This can be achieved by accentuating roles, instead of positions, combined with establishing a decentralized, cell-structure-based organizational model, and by establishing consultative, individual decision-making for decisions beyond the team level.

All of these characteristics can be observed in the best organizations: Those featuring the highest overall levels of self-organization, such as Handelsbanken, Toyota, dm-drogerie markt, Southwest Airlines, or W.L.Gore. These company cases beautifully highlight that self-organization, in organizational reality, must always be combined with the principle of decentralization of decision making towards roles and teams in the organizational periphery.

In other words: Decentralization and self-organization are the two sides of the same coin. This illustrates why frameworks and methods that supposedly "produce" self-organization – from blockchain to holacracy – are actually inapt and unlikely to significantly contribute to it. The cases of real-world, large-scale, long-term self-organized companies, on the other hand, prove that the future of (self)organization is already here. It is just unevenly distributed.

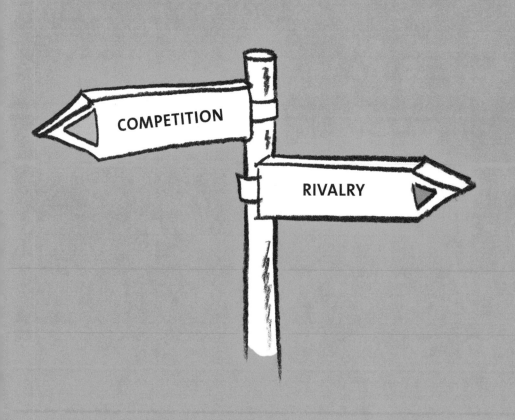

COMPETITION IN ORGANIZATIONS: IS IT GOOD, OR IS IT BAD?

This question is wrong.

Competition within organizations is neither good, nor bad. Whether internal competition is useful, constructive and appropriate depends on the level to which we let it happen, or on how it is stimulated or suppressed. In other words: there is an organizational domain where competition is good, and where it makes sense. There is another domain in organizations, however, where competition will inevitably turn dysfunctional, toxic, vicious and destructive.

In many organizations, as most of us are aware, competition on the level of the individual is actively stimulated and incentivized. This is usually done through performance management tools such as individual target setting ("MbO," "quotas," "goals," "OKRs"), individual incentives linked into these targets ("bonuses," "premiums"), and individual performance "appraisal." Often, techniques such as "feedback" and "coaching" are also thrown into the mix. We might call this the command-and-control type of competition, more specifically it is a form of steering, of fear-inducing individualization, or top-down-driven rivalry.

In organizations, individual performance does not even exist. Here, performance emerges in the space between people. That is the nature of the organization.

All of this is not only dreadful practice; it is destructive. The fundamental reason why these tools and practices do not actually work is this: Individual performance, in organizations, does not exist. The notion of individual performance is a crude over-simplification of organizational reality, performance is not something that individuals within an organization can do, or create by themselves. Instead, performance in organizations always happens in the space between people. It arises from interactions between individuals, or from "performing with-each-other-for each-other" – which is an expression we discovered at dm-drogerie markt a little more than a decade back.

The collective, interdependent nature of work and value creation in companies as well as in not-for-profits is not an option. It is part of organizational physics. This becomes ever more obvious in complex, dynamic, and globalized markets.

This insight about the nature of organizational performance leads us to the "good kind" of competition in organizations. It is competition (not: rivalry!) among teams, not individuals. It is when teams are set up as functionally integrated, highly autonomous, self-organized, self-steering, that they can actually compete for business results. This is a far cry, of course, from the misery that is usually instilled in today´s functionally differentiated command-and-control silos, such as "Sales." This healthy kind of competition works, as the long-running examples of companies such as Handelsbanken and dm-drogerie markt have shown.

Given the interdependent nature of value creation, individuals within an organization cannot actually compete with each other. They can only be rivals.

Healthy competition depends on a set of principles natural to self-organization. It works if it happens among self-steering teams capable of running themselves like mini-enterprises, and without the disadvantages of rivalry or the bane of centralized steering.

LET SELF-STEERING, FUNCTIONALLY INTEGRATED TEAMS COMPETE –
not individuals!

Prerequisites are as follows:

› Firstly, measuring of performance must end at the team level, and should never happen reach to the individual level. Because the team is the smallest possible unit of performance in an organization.

› Secondly, Performance measures on the team level must focus on relative performance, not on fixed targets. Relative measures ma include "Return on Sales as a %, compared to average" or "Cost/Income Ratio, over time", instead of numbers fixed in advance, such as "Sales of 10.000 units," "Growth of 7%."

› Neither team nor team members should be incentivized monetarily. Ever.

Functional integration will make your silos, departments, business areas and matrix structures go away. And pave the way for team-based competition that works.

But perhaps the most startling prerequisite for healthy, constructive and empowering competition among self-steering teams may, at this point, be functional integration. This is because we have become incredibly used to functional division, or separation of functions into departments, areas, units and silos. Most of us think of functional division as "normal." We find it hard to imagine a structure in which groups of, say, 5 to 8 people run a small, intra-company business together, in the shape of a highly autonomous team that would perform most of the various functions of their business themselves. Functions as diverse as marketing, making proposals to clients, selling, delivering, servicing, billing – with just the occasional service from the organizational center, on an as-needed basis.

Functional integration not only allows organizations to induce healthy team competition, while averting dysfunctional side effects. It also always leads to the elimination of functional silos such as Sales, Operations, or conventional Business Units. In fact, functional integration always goes hand in hand with complexity-robustness in the shape of federative, decentralized, team-based organizational design. This is worth achieving these days.

Let the competition begin!

THE MCGREGOR PARADOX.
THE MOST TRAGIC MISUNDERSTANDING IN THE HISTORY OF WORK AND ORGANIZATIONS

A few months ago, a student from Germany asked me how it came that I was "pretty much the only one" passionately and repeatedly claiming that Theory X people do not exist. The student suggested that I was probably mistaken with my interpretation of Douglas McGregor's work, and with my interpretation of human nature at work as such. I had to be mistaken, she said, because everybody else's writing on McGregor hinted at what I so passionately denied: Those "Xers" – they exist in organizations. Her professor at the university also said so, she told me.

With just a touch of drama, I replied that even if I were the only person on earth to argue that Theory X people do not exist at all (which I am not!) I would still be the true heir of McGregor. Not those others! I told her that, clearly, not many people had actually cared to read McGregors original book, *The Human Side of Enterprise*, published back in 1960. And that, apparently, even those who had read it had not done so carefully enough to pick up the actual message. McGregor was saying it on pretty much every page of his book.

Theory Xers do not exist. Have never existed, will never exist. Theory X is just an ugly prejudice about other people at work.

I told the student that flawed interpretations of McGregors insight have been so notorious, since the original publication of the book back in the 60s, that even the celebratory "Annotated Edition" contains comments from renown academic "followers" of McGregor claiming the exact opposite of McGregor's insight, arguing: *"Well, yes, those Theory X people exist."* The problem, I believe, lies in what I have come to call the McGregor Paradox:

In management textbooks today, McGregor is usually depicted as a "motivational researcher who did not back up his claims on human nature with robust research and evidence." This is the most ludicrous claim, given that McGregor's crucial insight is of a philosophical, quasi-physical nature, applied to the realm of organizational, and business sciences. Imagine somebody saying: "Ah, Newton's work on gravity. Good stuff. But where is the serious quantitative evidence or research to back it up? Why did he not do that? That's why I don't´ buy it: The guy did not even present proof!" Or think of this: *"Yeah, Einstein's Relativity Theory. It is quite interesting – but my personal experience tells me differently, you know!"*

What I said to the student is: "The question is not if Xers exist. That is actually a no-brainer, but sadly, 95% of supposed business experts, thought leaders, and academics, are quacks. Here is why:

The problem seems to be that close to 60 years after McGregor's insight, most so-called experts still claim, and believe, that Theory Xers exist. They say it. They teach it. They act according to a myth that McGregor should have effectively dispelled in 1990. They apply methods that could only possibly work with Xers, even though, as I will emphasize again on behalf of McGregor, Xers not exist at all. How would you call that?"

The student was skeptical, of course, with regards to my arguments. So I told her to pick up a copy of The Human Side of Enterprise and see for herself. A week or so later the student got back to me. She apologized. Admitted that everything I had told her about McGregor's book was actually there, loud and clear, impossible to overlook, even. And that it made total sense. She said it was now obvious to her that McGregor had based the entire book on the crucial insight that Theory X human nature assumptions are a fraud. It was clear to her now that pretty much everyone since The Human Side of Enterprise had misquoted, even abused McGregor's original message about Xers and Yers. She acknowledged to be somewhat puzzled about that fact. And that bewilderment is a feeling I share.

"Believers" of Theory X find it hard to acknowledge McGregor's message, even if it is pushed in their faces. Their own beliefs blind them to reality and insight.

Even six decades after McGregor's book, we are still stuck in a world of Theory X delusion. Never mind those days before McGregor: Maybe we could not know we were wrong. It was an age of innocence! But when McGregor finally told us, we should have listened. We should have learned. But, by and large, we did not. Most of us are guilty of perpetuating the Theory X prejudice. It is the biggest tragedy in the history of work, and organizations. It is a humanistic scandal, as it leads to a horrible waste of human potential, as well as to abuse of people, organizations, and power. It may be the biggest fraud in history.

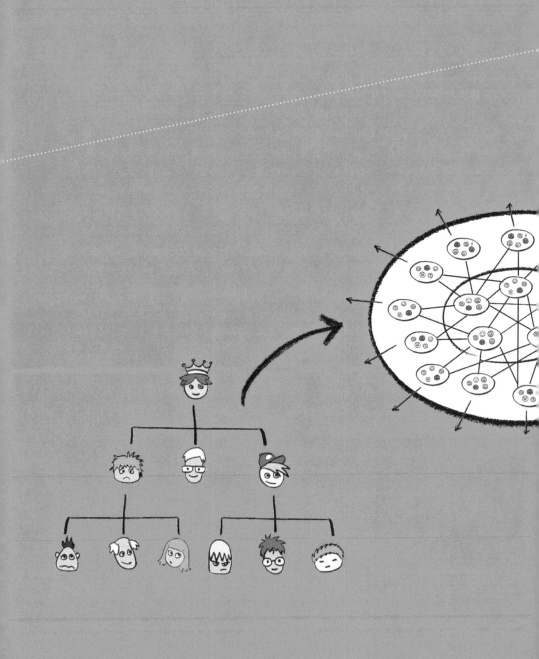

FIVE SECRETS OF VERY FAST ORGANIZATIONAL TRANSFORMATION (VFOT)

Most managers today, most change agents and people in organizations doubt that something like organizational transformation is possible at all, at least not within their particular company, or organization. If they do not reject the idea outright, they figure that it would take forever to make serious transformation of the organizational model happen. "It would take years or decades! We are not ready for that." That was the predominant belief until this day. We hold a rather different perspective on transformation: one that we will outline in this article. We firmly believe, and indeed know, that profound organizational transformation is possible in any company, anywhere. We also hold that when it happens, it can happen fast – within just a few months.

The secret to Very Fast Organizational Transformation, in companies large or small, old or new, local or global, lies in appropriately complex, robust transformation methods, or approaches. Such approaches now exist. Not only that: they are open source and available to all. This insight was not pulled out of thin air. The new breed of fast, and highly practical approaches to Very Fast Organizational Transformation, such as OpenSpace Beta (developed by Silke Hermann and myself in 2018) and OpenSpace Agility (developed by Daniel Mezick and others in 2015), hinges on several foundational sources and movements that have existed for quite a long time:

›   OpenSpace Beta applies insights from more than 20 years of BetaCodex Network/Beyond Budgeting case research and concept development that started back in 1998. Since then, it has taken into account insight from sciences as varied as business administration, psychology, organizational development and sociology. OpenSpace Beta is also inspired by the Lean and Agile movements, and original research on Beta concepts such as *Relative Performance Systems, OrgPhysics* and *Change-as-Flipping*, which are outlined in this book.

›   OpenSpace Agility applies insight from Scrum and Agile concepts, implementations and movements. Idealized some 20 years back, Scrum, for instance, has been applied in software development and beyond, worldwide, but it has also often fallen short of expectations, due to feeble, un-systemic, "industrialized" adoption techniques.

›   Both OpenSpace Beta and OpenSpace Agility make use of systems theory and cybernetics advanced by pioneers such as Kurt Lewin, Mary Parker Follett, Eric Trist, W. Edwards Deming, Russell Ackoff, Niklas Luhmann, Ernst Weichselbaum and others. These pioneers contributed to our understanding of how to effectively set up & irritate organizational systems.

›   Both VFOT approaches derive their conceptual architecture
    from the Prime OS social technology, which was developed by
    Daniel Mezick and others, a few years back.

›   They both employ OpenSpace, the large-group interaction for-
    mat that was idealized by Harrison Owen in the early 1980s.

›   They build upon whole-systems approaches advanced by
    organizational development sages such as Marvin Weisbord,
    Paul Tolchinsky, Kathie Dannemiller and Bill Pasmore, who pio-
    neered, among many things, the use of large-group techniques
    and OpenSpace derivatives in organizations, from the 1990s
    onwards.

The two VFOT approaches have been outlined in separate hand-
books, or practical guides, that allow readers to make transformation happen within any organization you might be part of, or
with your clients. But how does this new kind of approach change
or transform work at all? What makes it different from ordinary
change management, change leadership, or known systemic approaches to organizational development?

The answer is five-fold.

PRINCIPLE 1
PRINCIPLED, NOT AMBIGUOUS

The best, most practical organizational theories are principle-based. Very Fast Organizational Transformation cannot be
brought about if the underlying content, aim, or practical theory
is not principle-based. The kind of practical theories we are talking

about do not promote prescriptions, rules, tools, or mere "best practices." They are not vague or esoteric. They are not mechanistic frameworks. The distinct feature of principle-based theory is that it can at the same time be specific, while not pre-defining a solution before it exists in a specific context, or organization (see page 12). This is because principles, by nature, must be interpreted by groups of humans. What makes principled approaches so powerful, durable and robust? They must be constantly socialized, or agreed within the specific social group that wish to adhere to them. Examples of principle-based practical theories, or social technologies are:

› LEAN, OR TOTAL QUALITY (TQM) – when applying the 14 key principles by W. Edwards Deming, for example.

THE LAWS OF BETA (DO THIS!) -
versus the Laws of Alpha (Not that!)

LAW	DO THIS!	NOT THAT!
01. Team autonomy	Connectedness with purpose,	not dependency
02. Federalization	Integration into cells,	not division into silos
03. Leaderships	Self-organization,	not management
04. All-around success	Comprehensive fitness,	not mono-maximization
05. Transparency	Flow intelligence,	not power obstruction
06. Market orientation	Relative Targets,	not top-down prescription
07. Conditional income	Participation,	not incentives
08. Presence of mind	Preparation,	not planned economy
09. Rhythm	Tact & groove,	not fiscal-year orientation
10. Mastery-based decision	Consequence,	not bureaucracy
11. Resource discipline	Expedience,	not status-orientation
12. Flow coordination	Value-creation dynamics,	not static allocation

› QUICK RESPONSE MANUFACTURING (QRM) – when applying the 10 QRM principles articulated by Rajan Suri.

› AGILE – when applying the 4+12 principles from the Agile Manifesto, or the principles embedded in the Scrum Guide.

› BETA – featuring the 12 principles of the BetaCodex, which were derived, in 2007, from the principles of the Beyond Budgeting model.

As an illustration of what such organizational principles look and feel like, take the principles of the BetaCodex. These principles are called "laws," and the full set of laws of Beta is depicted on the left.

Principle-based, practical theories such as Beta, Lean, QRM or Agile come with twists. For instance, they are all indivisible, by nature. Which means that their sets of principles are not menus to choose from. The principles are clearly interdependent, even if it may not appear like that, at first glance. Additionally, in order to agree on principles, or to socialize them, a certain level of awareness of group participants, or a certain level of willingness to face conflict with peers are indispensable.

Principled practical theory allows us to be focused & specific, while refraining from the foolishness of pre-defining solutions within complex contexts. Challenges: Such theory is indivisible; it must be constantly socialized within a group.

In other words: Principles are the only way, and the natural way, to convey the nature of complex systems to social groups, large and small. Which is why manifestos, constitutions, or statements of intent are usually articulated through principles. Principled practical theory will provide an indispensable type of boundary to Very Fast Organizational Transformation, contributing to the robustness and the reliability of the process, as well as enabling self-organization and emergence.

This concept provides a second kind of boundary to Very Fast Organizational Transformation: Boundaries in time. We grasped this concept more fully through Daniel Mezick´s pioneering work around OpenSpace Agility. Daniel figured this out some years ago, in the context of helping organizations with adopting Scrum as a work method for teams. Scrum, of course, relies heavily on time-boxing, or setting boundaries of time. So it seemed natural to apply this concept not just to work within the system but to work on the system.

The insight here is quite intuitive, really: We should always time-box (or: "restrict") periods of time during which specific organizational development work is supposed to take place. This way, we do not artificially fix the scope of the work, but the time allocated. Combined with principle-based theory, participants in the change work will experience a sense of safety and reliability through time-boxing, even throughout phases of disruption. Daniel Mezick had the idea of time-boxing the change work, or giving it rhythm, by "starting in OpenSpace and ending in OpenSpace," and allocating a period of roughly three months, in-between.

The problem with the assumption that "change takes a lot of time" is that it annihilates the possibility of working the organizational system when it is needed.

Let´s remember: Based on their past experiences in the context of work, most managers or employees in larger companies will naturally assume that change usually drags on, endlessly! Consequently, something like profound transformation would, in this mindset, inevitably take years or even decades! In other words: Change is all too often perceived as hard, slow and overwhelming (in addition to it being forced upon the many by the few).

The problem with the assumption of change taking a lot of time and change work not having a specific horizon in time is that it annihilates the possibility for working on the organizational system, not just within the system when it is needed. As humans in social groups, we cannot focus our collective energy well within undefined, vague time-spaces. This trait of social groups invalidates indefinite, or long-term phases of change. *"We will sort out that strategy issue during the next six months,"* or *"We will reduce cost over the next 18 months"* – such statements are predictions of their own failure. Humans need to be capable of seeing the horizon. This creates safety. It creates conditions for peer pressure and a sense of orientation.

The paradigm-shift comes with changing the mental model: "Transformation does not take forever. If we time-box the transformation to, say, 90 days increments, then it will take exactly 90 days!

When organizational development work is principled, inclusive (more about that later) and time-boxed, then transformation is turned into a joint rite of passage. This means that it will be ritualized, with a clear and evident beginning and end, with iterations set by rituals. In OpenSpace Beta, for instance, a full chapter of approximately 180 days contains a total of five iterations, at least. Look at the Open-Space Beta time-line on the following double page, and you will be able to spot them.

The first 60 days of *Build-up* clearly is the first iteration, in itself. *OpenSpace Meeting 1* is another, then there are the 90 days of *Practicing-Flipping-Learning* as the core iteration, or as a "large sprint," followed by the "large retrospective" of *OpenSpace Meeting 2*, which may count as iteration number four, before the closing iteration of the 30-day *Quiet Period*. Within a roughly 180-day time frame, OpenSpace Beta thus takes participants and teams through at least five major iterations. That may be followed by another OpenSpace Beta chapter that is structured along the same cadence.

THE OPENSPACE BETA TIME-LINE:
How to make organizational transformation happen in just a few months

Sponsor

Facilitator

Formally Authori
Managers

OPENSPACE ROLES

Participants

Conveners

Master
of ceremonies

60 DAYS

OPENSPACE
MEETING 1

BUILD-UP (SET STAGE!)

BEGINNING (PREPARE!)

PRACTIC

Preparing
executives

Day 1:
Opt-in meeting

Practicing
Beta team patter

Socializing the
invitation (45 days)

Theme
crafting

Day 2:
Prep day

BetaCodex
constraints

Coaching
role begins

Proceedings
OS 1

Draft & send
invitation

encers
tationers

Teams

BETA ROLES

OPENSPACE ROLES

hes

Stakeholders

DAYS

OPENSPACE MEETING 2

30 DAYS

NG – LEARNING (DO!)

ENDING (CHECK!)

QUIET PERIOD (LEVEL UP!)

:reation
:thening

Proprietors
of power in action

Day 1 & 2:
Opt-in meeting

Coaching
role ends

-boxed
)ing

Deliberate
storytelling

Chapter
debrief

ning
:ration

Theme
& invitation

Proceedings
OS 2

Recurring
OpenSpace

Time-boxing, combined with principled practical theory, helps social groups large and small to raise the energy level during the collaborative sprint period, and also to provide for a different energy during periods of looking back and ahead, allowing the same groups to engage in reflection and retrospective.

RADICALLY INVITING, NOT IMPOSING

This is another concept we got from Daniel Mezick, whose Open-Space Agility served as a foundation to OpenSpace Beta. This principle is delightfully simple, yet also quite novel in the context of organizational development. You start with everyone who wants to join in, by radically inviting them, while accepting that the invitation may be declined. This way, you will always start with the right people, those who are willing to engage at that particular time, by accepting the invitation.

Radical invitation or opt-in participation means the invitation can be declined without punishment. When an invitation is declined, you can never quite know why. You must keep inviting!

A key aspect of change management work is that they are most often forced upon people. Little wonder they usually fail! The language we use to describe change tells the whole story. We speak of status quo, kick-offs, roll-outs, getting in the boat, implementation, execution, convincing, aligning. If that does not work, we force and bribe those who are affected, crushing their resistance to change. The intent is to inflict solutions upon them which have previously been worked out by others. Look at the actual practices in change management approaches and you will see that, say, 95% of them are fundamentally imposition-based. This will always produce resistance against the change method, erode social density, provoke disengagement and de-motivation. The price of imposition is too high to ever be weighed!

Radical invitation or opt-in participation means the invitation can be declined without punishment. You can also opt out! What sounds like a problem really isn't. Because full engagement among those opting in will be the result. Those who accept will be the right people. *"An invitation accepted means the specific object of the invitation is wanted,"* Daniel Mezick once told us. *"When declined, you can never quite know why."* Which is why marveling about rejection of invitation is of little help. It is far better to make invitations very attractive. And to keep inviting.

PRINCIPLE 4
WHOLE-SYSTEM, NOT PIECE-MEAL

Over the last couple of years it has become somewhat fashionable to promote piece-meal transformation. Piece-meal approaches come in many shapes and varieties. As "slicing and dicing", for example, so that interventions will be applied to individual business units, departments, areas or functions only ("Agile HR" is an example). So called "pilots" and "labs" are usually no more than slicing and dicing, either. At present, most Lean, TQM, Scrum and Agile is applied by slicing and dicing, sadly. Piecemeal approaches, at first glance, seem to offer quick wins or low-hanging fruit. But, as many have learned the hard way and through expensive efforts, these approaches do not work, and cannot work, and for a simple reason: One cannot transform departments or functions (or: mere parts of a system) individually, because we will inevitably end up just dabbling within the system, instead of working on the system. Notions of experiments, hacks, or other forms of dabbling of course also fall short of transforming organizational models, or systems in a coherent and potentially lasting fashion.

Counter-intuitive insight: To produce profound change fast, we must take whole organizations into view – not slices, bits or pieces. By intervening on the whole system, or flipping the system, we can speed up transformation of organizations large & small to Very Fast.

What piece-meal, non-systemic change management, as well as tools, rules & frameworks do not take into account is that actual transformation requires:

› First producing insight among members of the system, or change of mental models of many,

› Then working the system, together, for behavioral patterns and iterations to actually adapt and change.

To make that happen, there must be a rite of passage that all members of the social system in question can pass through. There is no alternative to this "working-the-entire-system-together" approach. Otherwise you will end up trying to change people, or force behaviors upon people – while achieving little. The counter-intuitive

---

OPENSPACE   Five principles, one law

FIVE PRINCIPLES OF OPENSPACE

Whoever comes is the right people.
Whenever it starts is the right time.
When it's over, it's over.
Whatever happens is the only thing that could have.
Wherever it happens is the right place.

THE ONE LAW OF OPENSPACE

If at any time during our time together you find yourself in any situation where you are neither learning nor contributing, use your two feet and go to some more productive place.

---

insight here: We must take whole organizations into view to make profound change fast. Only by intervening on the whole system, or by flipping the system, consciously, can transformation of organizations large & small be sped up to Very Fast.

Another dimension of whole-system approaches is to include everyone, at the same time, early-on. This is very different than "scaling," phasing, slicing and dicing, or stacking involvement. While change management relies on having solutions developed behind closed doors first by chosen ones, then "rolling them out," Very Fast Organizational Transformation does the opposite: Inviting everyone at once to work the whole organization, together, based on a principled approach and through time-boxed iterations. Question is: How do you get everyone involved & engaged at once? Answer: You need an additional piece of social tech: An engagement model.

Question is: How do you get everyone involved and engaged at once? The answer: You need an additional piece of social technology: You need an "engagement model."

The engagement model that both OpenSpace Beta and OpenSpace Agility employ is of course the social technology called OpenSpace, which was already envisioned by Harrison Owen way back in the early 1980s, but which only now returns to its home turf of organizational development. OpenSpace itself is based on a total of six principles – it combines extreme simplicity of setup with radical self-organization. And it easily scales to a few thousand participants for a single event.

In the overview on the left, you can see what OpenSpace looks like, articulated through six principles, all in all, of which one is called "the one law."

Involvement of everyone up-front who accepts the invitation through an opt-in engagement model has several functions: It allows to build a shared mindset quickly, and then involve all the right people immediately to perform many, many interventions on system and interactions all at once. This is where the speed in VFOT comes from: Organizations exist so that many can share in the work. Why not develop the organization together, too?

Involvement of course works best when a couple of conditions are met, i.e. when the time-frame is restricted and when the effort is focused on a specific, principled purpose. Humans can commit more easily then. That is the very opposite of getting in the boat, convincing, aligning, or hustling people into action.

In this sense, Very Fast Organizational Transformation attempts the opposite of aiming at quick wins. While quick-win-approaches will always push the great achievement of the "real transformation" into the future, usually resulting in some quick wins and then nothing. VFOT adheres to the old Yoda adage: *Do, or do not – there is no try!*

So in order to get VFOT, you must really, really want it, first.

VERY FAST ORGANIZATIONAL TRANSFORMATION
LET´S MAKE IT OPEN AND AVAILABLE TO ALL

We believe that all social technology is born to be open source. We believe that social technologies are born to be open source. They should be available to all. Their creators should always be credited: It should be natural to build upon other´s creations and remix, tweak & develop further, while referencing the sources! Only if we set innovative social technologies free can we expect to solve the urgent problems of our time, together. Such problems as hopelessly outdated organizational models that infest our companies and workplaces, worldwide. Such problems as the dramatic lack of learning, development and advancement in organizations and in work.

authoritarian **democratic** **laissez-faire**

LEADERSHIP STYLES: THEY ARE NOT WHAT YOU THINK THEY ARE

In the late 1930s, the great Kurt Lewin was the first to distinguish different "leadership styles." Lewin´s classification identified the "authoritarian," the "democratic" and the "laissez-faire" styles. So far, so good.

But guess what: According to Lewin himself, two of these "styles" have nothing to do with leadership, really. Zip. Zero. Nothing.

There are not three leadership styles in Lewin´s distinction. There is only one. While the others are frequently mistaken for leadership.

Until this very day, there is more misunderstanding than understanding of the significance of Lewin´s crucial insight: Lewin was not actually exploring "three different, acceptable options for being a good, or decent leader." Instead, his distinction was a condemnation: Lewin was condemning all work interaction that was non-collaborative and non-democratic and that, at the time, was deemed "acceptable" by many. He did not think that everything was fine with leadership. According to his concept, there are not three leadership styles. There is only one leadership style – while the two other are frequently mistaken for leadership! Sadly, not much has changed in that regard.

PUT DIFFERENTLY:

› Leadership is not "situational." It never was! If you ever feel like stepping over into the domains of authoritarianism or laissez-faire, do not ask yourself who is wrong, but what in the system deserves fixing.

› We must put an end authoritarianism in organizations. Many of our societies have overcome authoritarianism, in the 20th century, but organizations have not. In the workplace, command-and-control is widely tolerated, and even deemed acceptable. That is a mistake. Autocracy and patriarchy – they do not bode businesses well in the 21st century.

› We must stay clear of laissez-faire. Laissez-faire is not "the opposite of authoritarianism." It is an entirely different evil. One that is pretty common in companies today, sadly.

› Transactional Leadership – that notion does not even make sense. It is an oxymoron, really! Its twin sibling, Transformational Leadership, on the other hand, is either meaningless or does not exist!

› Paternalism, a variety of authoritarianism, is always evil, too. Because people at work are not children!

OR, PUT QUITE BLUNTLY:

Now it is time to put autocratic and laissez-faire attitudes on the garbage heap of history. Let us stop hypocrisy at work. Lewin called us to do so, some 80 years ago. Since then, our societies have become far more democratic, while complexity has forced command-and-control onto its knees. Now is the time to actually put autocratic and laissez-faire attitudes on the garbage heap of history.

We are 80 years late already.

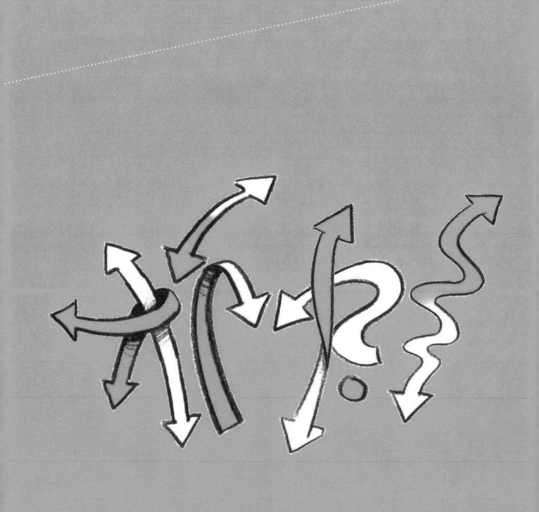

BOSSES VS. LEADERS: COMPANIES NEED NEITHER!

I once saw an illustration on my news stream on LinkedIn, about the differences between "the boss" and "the leader." Most of us have probably seen this kind of visual many times before: They invariably argue for "bosses becoming more like leaders;" for "leaders becoming more transformational," and/or for companies to not have bosses altogether. Let´s look at this line of thinking a little bit closer.

The first thing that may come to mind is that both bosses and leaders are supposedly about work and relationships between human beings, but that people, in the kind of visual seen below, are usually portrayed as animals. In this case, people are cast as sheep

People need not be given credit — they are not dogs.

on the left, and as fish on the right. Which in itself is kind of insightful. In other visuals on the topic of leadership, we often find flocks of birds and swarms of ants used as metaphors for humans. Which is just as inspiring.

Dah.

But let's take a closer look at the text in the visual below. The left side obviously appears as quite dreadful and is outlined as some

A TALE OF SHEEP AND FISHES
found on LinkedIn

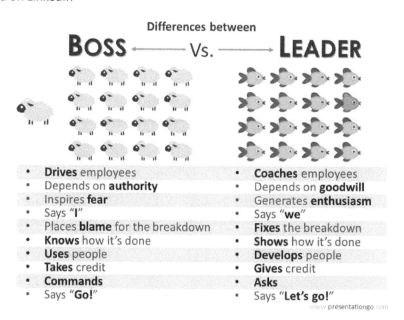

Differences between

Boss ——— Vs. ——— Leader

- **Drives** employees
- Depends on **authority**
- Inspires **fear**
- Says "**I**"
- Places **blame** for the breakdown
- **Knows** how it's done
- **Uses** people
- **Takes** credit
- **Commands**
- Says "**Go!**"

- **Coaches** employees
- Depends on **goodwill**
- Generates **enthusiasm**
- Says "**we**"
- **Fixes** the breakdown
- **Shows** how it's done
- **Develops** people
- **Gives** credit
- **Asks**
- Says "**Let's go!**"

www.presentationgo.com

sort of reign of terror. Which it is. But is the notion of "leaders" developed on the right side really so much better? I don´t think so. In fact, pretty much all assumptions made in the illustration are highly problematic in the context of work, people and organizations. For instance:

› PEOPLE CANNOT ACTUALLY BE COACHED FROM THE TOP – coachees either choose their coaches on a voluntary basis, or it is not "coaching" at all!

› PEOPLE AT WORK DON´T NEED SOMEONE WHO GENERATES ENTHUSIASM – that sounds more like constant pep talking, or like happy slavery.

› PEOPLE DON´T NEED SOMEONE WHO SAYS "WE" – it is outright obvious that a company, a firm or organization is not about individuals, but about creating-value-for-others-together with others.

› PEOPLE DO NOT NEED FIXERS OF BREAKDOWNS – they are not children.

› PEOPLE NEED NOT BE DEVELOPED – they can do that themselves.

› PEOPLE NEED NOT BE GIVEN CREDIT – they are not dogs.

› PEOPLE DO NOT NEED SOMEONE WHO ASKS – they are able to think for themselves if we let them, and literally everyone should ask questions

› PEOPLE NEED NOT HEAR "LET´S GO" FROM SOMEONE WITHIN THE ORGANIZATION – there is always a customer for whom value is created.

Ultimately, the song of the *Transformational Leader*, the *Great Leader*, or the *Level 5 Leader* is always about one ugly thing: Blaming.

The closer one observes the "be a leader" propaganda, the more apparent it becomes that being a leader is not about leadership at all: It is still about dependency, steering, and command-and-control.

Watch even closer, and you will find that, ultimately, the song of the "transformational leader," the "great leader," or "Level 5 leader" is inevitably about blaming. It is about blaming today´s managers for being either too stupid, too busy or too unwilling to lead their sheep- or fish-like people, so that the flocks stay out of trouble.

In short: The left side and the right side – they are both fundamentally, and utterly flawed. The notion of the leader is and has always been corrupt and despicable, just as the notion of bosses. Or put differently: If we think of leadership as depending on leaders & followers, or of leaders as "very special people," then we haven´t advanced a bit from what Frederick W. Taylor told us about managing for the industrial age, over 100 years ago, in his treatise *Principles of Scientific Management*.

PEOPLE ARE NEITHER SHEEP,
NOR FISH.

Leadership happens in the space between people when market-driven self-organization is unleashed. It is not the job of bosses who may have been re-baptized as "leaders"!

So let´s end the hypocrisy. Together. And allow our organizations to become much more high-performing in the process.

CRAZY. STUPID. LEARNING. THE TWO TYPES OF LEARNING AND WHY BOTH MATTER

To organize for complexity also means to organize learning and development for complexity – on the individual, the team and the organizational level. Much has been said and written in recent years about learning in organizations and business schools. Much of this talk has been based on flawed assumptions.

Applying one of the thinking tools from my book *Organize for Complexity* may help to figure out how we can improve conditions and settings for learning, and maybe even create the high level of learning that Peter Senge and many of us have been dreaming of for decades.

The "thinking tool" I like to use for this (seen below) offers a distinction that many of you have probably heard about. But I believe the consequences are frequently misunderstood.

FROM DATA TO MASTERY
The two types of learning

DATA	INFORMATION	KNOWLEDGE	MASTERY
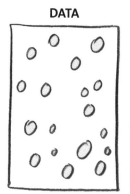	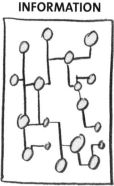	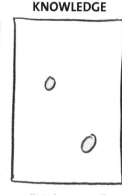	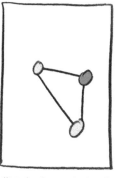
		"Make sense"	"Make knowledge"

Let's use the distinction shown here — between Data, Information, Knowledge and Mastery — to reflect on how the transformation from one into the other works:

› THE FIRST IS TRANSFORMING DATA INTO INFORMATION. This is in the domain of "IT" (not learning). To do this, you do not need humans, nor are they necessarily involved.

› TRANSFORMING INFORMATION INTO KNOWLEDGE
("I2K" LEARNING): It is here where things get interesting, as
knowledge involves humans, and human activity. This "I2K"
transformation is the domain of "personal, or individual
learning." Some call this "basic" learning. Learners or students
can practice this kind of learning individually, from home,
on-line etc. When you look up something on Wikipedia, watch a
TED video, read a book or article, or search for something on
Google, it´s this kind of learning that occurs.

› TRANSFORMING KNOWLEDGE INTO MASTERY
("K2M" LEARNING) is a second way of learning: the domain of
"collective learning" so to speak. It is one that requires learners
to practice with each other, or to practice together with "mas-
ters" (i.e. someone with mastery). One might say that here, you
need at least two learners! This "K2M" transformation can
happen in the classroom, "on the job," by practicing problem-solving, by seeking advice, or in direct on-line interaction.

While the first kind of learning, "I2K," is sufficient to make sense
and to solve known problems, the second kind is key to solving new
problems, and to deal effectively with complexity. It is "K2M"
learning that is needed for innovation and problem-solving in
dynamic markets. Unfortunately, of course, today´s MBA programs
mostly offer mere I2K learning to their students – the
case study method and business simulations not-
withstanding. Corporate conferences, leadership
development programs and organizational development activities are loaded with dispiriting I2K
presenting and contribute nothing to the development of mastery.

**"I2K" learning:
sufficient to solve known
problems. Insufficient for
solving problems in the
realm of complexity.**

What is the consequence of all of this, then? In order to create
effective development and learning spaces in higher education, in

organizational development and at conferences, we should leave basic "I2K" learning to where it belongs: pre-readings, online classes, MOOCs, YouTube etc. And we should create space for Knowledge-to-Mastery learning in classrooms and in our organizations. For example:

› "FLAT", CONVERSATIONAL, DISCOURSE-ORIENTED CLASSROOM SETTINGS. Instead of the "sage-on-the-stage" approach and lecturing.

› NO POWERPOINT, NO PRESENTING. Focusing live learning situations and classrooms on dialog, questioning and peer-to-peer exchange; using flip charts and other non-static documentation devices to let the content emerge throughout the interaction.

› KNOWLEDGE ACQUISITION AHEAD OF PRACTICING. Pre-readings, on-line learning, and on-line media should complement the setting in which everyone is present together, ideally ahead of the live learning encounter.

Settings in which learners and teacher meet in the same physical location are the most precious. Such settings should always focus on K2M learning .

› REFLECTIONS ON LEARNING. Self-reflection by learners about their learning at the end of each cycle, instead of knowledge testing, grading, or exams that end up getting in the way of learning.

TOWARDS MUCH BETTER USE OF CLASSROOMS AND GATHERINGS

Let´s liberate the college classroom, the MBA, corporate gatherings and Organizational Development from the boredoms of lecturing, presenting and frontal teaching! Let´s put technology to good use where it belongs (which is often I2K), and use valuable face-to-face time for high engagement settings, socially dense interaction and peer-to-peer learning. Technology can help us to liberate the workshop, the classroom, the course and the conference from I2K learning – so that we can make way better use of the live encounter.

I have found few practical and theoretically sound approaches that are in sync with this insight of two-fold learning, unfortunately. Some that I found are those by

› José Bowen (president at Goucher College, in the US), in his neat book *Teaching Naked*. Highly recommended!

› Peter Lorange (owner and president of Lorange Institute of Business Zurich, where I have also taught) in his many publications on how to reinvent the business school.

› Harold Jarche and others from the Internet Time Alliance who focus on corporate learning or learning in organizations. Jay Cross, an expert and writer on "informal learning" was also a member of this group, until his untimely death in 2015.

THINKING TOOLS: MANAGEMENT VS LEADERSHIP

THE MIGHTY DIFFERENCE BETWEEN THE TWO CONCEPTS.
Dedicated to Warren Bennis, 1925–2014

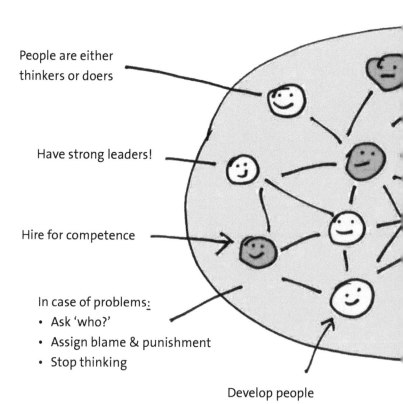

**MANAGEMENT:
Improve the parts!**

People are either
thinkers or doers

Have strong leaders!

Hire for competence

In case of problems:
- Ask 'who?'
- Assign blame & punishment
- Stop thinking

Develop people

LEADERSHIP:
Improve the interactions!

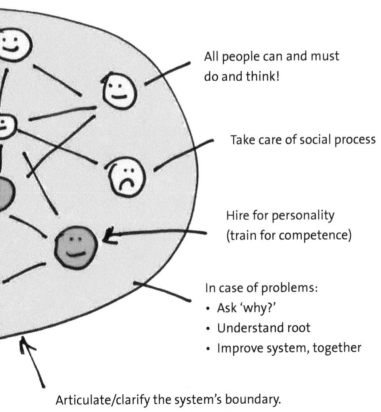

All people can and must
do and think!

Take care of social process

Hire for personality
(train for competence)

In case of problems:
- Ask 'why?'
- Understand root
- Improve system, together

Articulate/clarify the system's boundary.
Work the system, not the people

DIFFERENCES THAT MAKE A DIFFERENCE!

Words can blind us – or they can make us see.

Most of the time, we are not fully aware that the words we use are loaded with meaning: Which is why it makes a hell of a difference whether we are talking about teaching or learning. About goals or direction. About feedback or dialogue.

Here are a few differences that really make a difference on how we perceive the world we live in.

If you do not distinguish between education and training, you will only see costs.

If you do not distinguish between practicing and cramming, you will only see effort.

If you do not distinguish between knowledge and mastery, you will only see competence.

"To observe means making distinctions"
Niklas Luhmann

If you do not distinguish between errors and mistakes, you will only see failure.

If you do not distinguish between docility and wisdom, you will only see arrogance.

If you do not distinguish between experience and insight, you will only see age.

If you do not distinguish between trainings and training, you will only see instruction.

If you do not distinguish between teaching and learning, you will only see lecturing.

If you do not distinguish between training and learning, you will only see teachers.

If you do not distinguish between personnel development and development, you will only see programming.

If you do not distinguish between targets and direction, you will only see appraisal.

If you do not distinguish between measurement and reality, you will only see surfaces.

If you do not distinguish between culture and systems,
you will only see shadow plays.

If you do not distinguish between intentions and strategies,
you will only see planning.

If you do not distinguish between steering and leadership,
you will only see hierarchy.

If you do not distinguish between leading and leadership,
you will only see managing.

If you do not distinguish between self-organization and
laissez-faire, you will only see chaos.

If you do not distinguish between guard rails
and creating conditions, you will only see commands.

If you do not distinguish between trusting and confiding,
you will only see risk.

If you do not distinguish between complicated and complex,
you will only see problems.

*"One can state, without exaggeration, that the observation of and the search
for similarities and differences are the basis of all human knowledge."* **Alfred Nobel**

If you do not distinguish between motivation and motivating,
you will only see carrots and sticks.

If you do not distinguish between people and behavior,
you will only see resistance.

If you do not distinguish between planning and preparation,
you will only see activity.

If you do not distinguish between delegating and decentralizing,
you will only see dependency.

If you do not distinguish between autonomy and freedom, you will only see anarchy.

If you do not distinguish between a group and a team, you will only see crowds.

"Nothing works without distinction and designation. Not even nothing."
Niklas Luhmann

If you do not distinguish between responsibility and accountability, you will only see irresponsibility.

If you do not distinguish between top-down and outside-in, you will only see centralization.

If you do not distinguish between roles and positions, you will only see activity.

If you do not distinguish between equality and fairness, you will only see neediness.

If you do not distinguish between ideas and innovation, you will only see hype.

If you do not distinguish between incentives and profit sharing, you will only see donkeys.

If you do not distinguish between machine intelligence and human intelligence, you will only see dangerous robots.

If you do not distinguish between digitalization and progress, you will only see tech funding.

If you do not distinguish between consultation and exculpation, you will only see discouragement.

If you do not distinguish between analysis and understanding, you will only see blaming.

If you do not differentiate between wanting and managing,
you will only see bureaucracy.

If you do not differentiate between feedback and dialog,
you will only see helplessness.

If you do not distinguish between socializing and announcing,
you will only see coercion.

If you do not distinguish between change and intervention,
you will only see symptoms.

If you do not distinguish between invitation and instruction,
you will only see change management.

If you do not distinguish between managers and management,
you will only see culprits.

If you do not distinguish between alpha and beta,
you will only see optimization.

7 REASONS WHY THE DIGITAL TRANSFORMATION IS OVER-HYPED

It seems like everyone is putting out some sort of theory on "Digital Transformation" these days – whether we want them or not. So much is being aired about this supposed revolution, and related phenomena such as digital business models, new work, and A.I. that I found it hard to keep watching the debate from the sidelines. So here is my take on the topic:

7 reasons why the Digital Transformation is over-hyped.

THERE IS NO SUCH THING AS A DIGITAL TRANSFORMATION.
PERIOD.

What is currently happening, instead, is a continuation of the automation movement that began in the industrial age. This movement now increasingly turns to dramatically increased, internet-based connectivity.

REASON 2
MACHINE INTELLIGENCE DIFFERS FROM HUMAN INTELLIGENCE.

Machine intelligence is limited to the domain of the complicated, or the Blue. Within the domain of the Blue, machines can actually outperform human beings. When that happens (e.g. when chess machine Deep Blue beat Garry Kasparov in 1997, or when Go computer AlphaGo beat Lee Sedol in 2016), people frequently react with awe and proceed to create myths around those machines' supposedly disruptive potential.

In work and in value creation, the Blue and the Red shake hands.

The Blue is not the only domain there is, however. There is also the domain of the Red, or the complex. This matters, because in work and value creation, the Blue and the Red shake hands. In work and in organizations, the domains of the complicated and the complex are both present.

Fortunately, and contrary to machines, human beings are capable of acting within both domains: the Blue and the Red. They can deal with both the complicated and the complex. Why? Because humans are capable of dealing with surprise – something that machines are not. This becomes apparent from a crucial ability that people have, but that no machine has: the ability to have ideas.

THE DOMAINS OF THE BLUE AND THE RED:
A difference that makes a difference

complicated	complex
formal, fixed	dynamic
dead	alive
repetition	surprise
machine	man

rules	principles
standards, processes	people with mastery
How does it work?	Who can do it?
top-down	outside-in
"push"	"pull"
permanent	temporary
formal structure	flow
targets	options
routines, commands	communication, dialog
industriousness, diligence	ideas, creativity

liberate procedure from people	integrate people and procedure
bosses	social density
bureaucracy	group pressure
hierarchical steering	market-driven self-organization
top-down control	team-based social control
power from controlling information	transparency
decisions	agreements
accountability	responsibility

Ideas are the stuff that matters in complexity: They connect the dots. Ideas are needed to solve any problem that possess a dose of Red.

The notion that machines may eventually cross the chasm into the Red belongs into the realm of fiction. It should be noted that if machines eventually were capable of having ideas, that would not matter to us humans at all: Humans would be dead immediately (as exemplified by sci-fi ancestors Skynet, or HAL 9000).

MACHINE INTELLIGENCE AND ABILITY TO SOLVE BLUE PROBLEMS ARE IMPORTANT TO ORGANIZATIONS. WHAT MATTERS MOST IS SOMETHING DECIDEDLY DIFFERENT, THOUGH.

In today´s markets, the ability to solve red problems is decisive. Companies need machine intelligence to compete for efficiency. The Achilles´ heel of most companies today, however, is not their lack of ability to make good use of machine intelligence, of processes, rules or standards (in other words to deal with blue problems), rather their general incapability to utilize human intelligence that is already available internally. In the presence of red problems, this inability to dig into human potential causes suffering in organizations and in work, everywhere in the world.

The Achilles´ heel of most organizations to-day: Their general inability to utilize internally available human intelligence.

This type of suffering from surprise and red problems is an inheritance from the industrial age: in the wide, slow-moving, dull mass markets of the past, the ability to solve blue problems was crucial for competing in the long run. Those days are gone! In dynamic, fast-moving, densely populated, global markets with strong competition, solving red problems has turned into the dominant competitive advantage. Any competitor´s idea today may become disruptive to your business tomorrow. Here, people with ideas become indispensable. Functionally divided structure, command-and-control, and division between thinkers and doers, however, stand in the way of smart, collective, agile human problem-solving.

Put differently: Companies these days appear to have technology issues. But those are just symptoms. In fact, the vast majority of organizations today has a profound structural problem: They are hooked on an organizational model that has long become obsolete and toxic.

REASONS 4 TO 7

Who the hell cares?

HEROES OF LEADERSHIP: THREE "FOUNDERS" OF ORGANIZATIONAL LEADERSHIP, ACKNOWLEDGED

All too often, we are unaware of the "heroes" of our field: The men and women who advanced organizational thinking in theory and practice. Most of the time, we fail to consider history, available science, and the systemic nature of work and organizations. I believe these founders of the field of organizational leadership and their insights matter to us today, and in a very practical sense. This article approaches the topic of leadership by looking at the achievements of three notable pioneers of organizational science, who all enriched and shaped the way we (should) perceive leadership today.

To understand what leadership is, and what leadership can be, it is worth having both available theory and history in mind. The history of organizational leadership begins at the time when large-scale corporations and the profession of management started to gain weight, at the height of the industrial age. Think railway corporations; think Ford´s Model T.

Let´s start with the man who began it all.

Frederick W. Taylor is, at the same time, hero and anti-hero in the story of leadership. He is considered, by some, the most influential figure in human history. Maybe rightly so. Management begins with Taylor – he was the one who defined its core characteristic and who thus consolidated the then nascent caste of management into a profession that was here to stay.

The guiding principle of hierarchically dividing the thinking from the doing, and then finding the optimal way to fulfill each task, outlined in his seminal book The Principles of Scientific Management, promoted previously unknown leaps in industrial efficiency and productivity. The division between thinking and doing became the defining principle of management per sé, shaping organizations, business education, work methods and practices everywhere, until this very day. Taylor´s approach became core content at Harvard Business School, and then business education everywhere. His quest for the one best way profoundly impacted life-style in the 20th century.

Taylor saw restriction of industrial output as a consequence of poor method, not worker inferiority. He thought that labor strife was not inevitable, and he spoke eloquently and passionately for labor-management cooperation – an ideal that his techniques could not support. Later-on, consultants, technocratic engineers and managers alike mastered Taylor´s method, and forgot the intent.

2. MARY PARKER FOLLETT (*1868 – †1933)

Mary Parker Follett was a pioneer in the field of human relations and democratic organization. Peter Drucker called her the "prophet of management" – meaning leadership, of course. Her contribution to the development of the field was in stark contrast to the scientific management theory of the early 1900's: Unlike efficiency engineers such as Taylor, and later behaviorists such as Elton Mayo who would attempt to "humanize" the command-and-control model, she argued for a human-relations approach that was decades ahead of its time.

Follett is increasingly recognized as the originator of ideas that are today commonly accepted as cutting edge in organizational theory.

These include the idea of seeking win-win solutions, strength in human diversity, and situational leadership. She stressed the interactions between managers and workers, presaging modern systems approaches. She was also a successful management consultant.

"To free the energies of the human spirit is the high potentiality of all human association."
Mary Parker Follett, the Leadership Sage

Follett was concerned about the misuse of the term leadership that had already become common in her time. In her definition, a leader was someone who sees the whole rather than the particular: "The best leader knows how to make his followers actually feel power themselves, not merely acknowledge his power." She was one of the first to integrate the idea of organizational conflict into leadership theory.

3. KURT LEWIN (*1890 – †1947)

Kurt Lewin pioneered the field of social psychology. His enormously influential body of work includes the creation or co-creation of concepts such as group dynamics, action research, experiential learning, and the understanding of the toxic effects of both autocratic and laissez-faire leadership styles. His Harwood experiments are the first recorded attempts at participative systems change through direct participation. Lewin sensed that tools mattered little in organizations, and that involving all stakeholders mattered a lot.

Lewin´s core principle of participation: we are more likely to carry out decisions we have helped make. This notion would evolve into the theory of participative management. Lewin thus added a new value to organizational leadership and development: democracy.

"You cannot understand a system until you try to change it."
Kurt Lewin, the Practical Theorist

The consistent theme in all of Kurt Lewin's work was his concern for the integration of theory and practice. This was expressed in his best-known quotation: "There is nothing so practical as a good theory."

It is a lesson we still need to internalize fully.

THINKING TOOLS: ORGANIZATIONAL HYGIENE

OVER THE LAST FEW DECADES, COMPANIES HAVE ADOPTED TONS OF NEW, FASHIONABLE METHODS AND TOOLS. THEY HAVE BECOME HOARDERS. The challenge today is that these once shiny tools are now standing in the way of consistent self-organization and "agility." Examples include performance appraisals, sales planning and quotas, budgeting and fixed targets, or concepts like Key Account Management, matrix structures, hiring processes and cost management, to name a few! Some of these tools and practices have ceased to work, due to context and constellations. Some never quite worked at all.

SPACE FOR YOUR NOTES
on Organizational Hygiene

"FAILED" PRACTICES YOU ARE AWARE OF
but that linger on:

STUFF YOU THINK IS USELESS BUT NOT HARMFUL
(though others may feel differently):

ORGANIZATIONAL HYGIENE MEANS "SPRING CLEANING" AN ORGANIZATION FROM FUTILE AND OBSTRUCTIVE PRACTICES AND TOOLS. But caution: Organizational practices will not "fade away," just because you wish for it. You have to consciously eliminate and abolish them. *Pick up the broom and the mop! Apply the disinfectant! Agree with everyone in your company about the end of all travel policies.* That is the work of Organizational Hygiene. Most companies have never done this sort of thing. That is like never, ever having freed your home from the dirty stuff that piles up, over time!

YOU SHOULD HAVE KILLED OFF THIS STUFF
a long time ago:

EXISTING PRACTICES YOU GREW SUSPICIOUS OF
while reading this book:

OVERVIEW OF SOURCES

1. *What is Beta?* Originally published on
    https://betacodex.org/about/laws/

2. *Why we cannot learn a damn thing from Toyota or Semco.*
    Originally published by Niels on his LinkedIn blog, 09/2015

3. *OrgPhysics. The 3 faces of every company: How a triad of
    structures allows companies to absorb complexity.*
    Originally published by Niels on his LinkedIn blog, 02/2017

4. *Flat hierarchies: They are just another step in the wrong
    direction.* Originally published by Niels on his LinkedIn blog,
    10/2016

5. *Change-as-Flipping: Change is more like adding milk to
    coffee.* Originally published by Niels on his LinkedIn blog,
    01/2015 and 04/2017 and as BetaCodex Network
    white paper No. 16

6. *Your company has exactly the culture it deserves.*
    Original translation for this collection. Adapted from an
    article published in German, in BankingNews 04/2015

7. *Abolish bonuses! There is no way around that.* Original trans-
    lation for this collection. Adapted from an article published
    in German in BankingNews 10/2014

8. *Bye-bye Management by Objectives! From Fixed to Relative
    Performance.* Originally published by Niels on his
    LinkedIn blog, 12/2014

9. *Social Density: The key to self-organization.*
    Originally published by Niels on his LinkedIn blog, 12/2017

10. *Competition in organizations: Is it good, or is it bad?* Originally published by Niels on his LinkedIn blog, 05/2017

11. *The McGregor Paradox. The most tragic misunderstanding in the history of work and organizations.* Originally published by Niels on his LinkedIn blog, 02/2018

12. *Five secrets of Very Fast Organizational Transformation (VFOT).* Originally published by Niels on his LinkedIn blog, 01/2019 and as BetaCodex Network white paper No. 16

13. *Leadership styles: They are not what you think they are.* Originally published by Niels on his LinkedIn blog, 06/2016

14. *Bosses vs. leaders: Companies need neither!* Originally published by Niels on his LinkedIn blog, 06/2016

15. *Crazy. Stupid. Learning. The 2 types of learning and why both matter.* Originally published by Niels on his LinkedIn blog, 12/2014

16. *Thinking tools: Management vs leadership.* Originally published by Niels on his LinkedIn blog, 05/2016

17. *Differences that make a difference.* Originally published by Niels on his LinkedIn blog on 25 June 2020

18. *7 reasons why the digital transformation is over-hyped.* Originally published by Niels on his LinkedIn blog, 07/2016

19. *Heroes of leadership: Three "founders," acknowledged.* Originally published by Niels on his LinkedIn blog, 01/2015

20. *Thinking tools: Organizational Hygiene.* Previously unpublished

RECOMMENDED READING

Bowen, José: *Teaching Naked – How Moving Technology Out of Your College Classroom Will Improve Student Learning.* Jossey-Bass, 2012

Bridges, William: *Managing Transitions – Making the Most of Change.* 25th anniversary edition, Da Capo Lifelong Books, 2017

Deutschman, Alan: *Change or Die – The Three Keys to Change at Work and in Life.* Harper Business, 2007

Graham, Pauline: *Mary Parker Follett – Prophet of Management.* HBRP, 1995

Kanigel, Robert: *The One Best Way – Frederick Winslow Taylor and the Enigma of Efficiency.* Viking Adult, 1997

Kotter, John: *Leading Change –* With a New Preface by the Author, 1R edition, HBRP, 2012

Marrow, Alfred Jay: *The Practical Theorist: The Life and Work of Kurt Lewin.* Basic Books, 1969

McGregor, Douglas: *The Human Side of Enterprise, annotated edition,* McGraw-Hill, 2005

Mezick, Daniel et al: *The OpenSpace Agility Handbook.* New Technology Solutions Inc., 2015

Owen, Harrison: *OpenSpace Technology – a user´s guide.* Berrett-Koehler Publishers, 2008

Pasmore, Bill: *Creating Strategic Change – Designing the Flexible, High-Performing Organization.* Wiley, 1994

Weisbord, Marvin: *Productive Workplaces – Dignity, Meaning, and Community in the 21st Century,* 3rd Edition. Pfeiffer, 2012

OTHER BOOKS FROM BETACODEX PUBLISHING

A POWERFUL NEW APPROACH TO FULL-FLEDGE
ORGANIZATIONAL TRANSFORMATION

Silke Hermann/Niels Pflaeginga
OpenSpace Beta.
A handbook for organizational transformation
in just 90 days
BetaCodex Publishing 2018.
Paperback/eBook. ISBN 978-0-9915376-6-2

THE MIND-BLOWING INTERNATIONAL BEST-SELLER!

Niels Pflaeging
Organize for Complexity.
How to get life back into work to build the
high-performance organization
4th edition. BetaCodex Publishing 2020.
Paperback/eBook. ISBN 978-0-9915376-0-0

BUSINESS THEORY AND PRACTICE FOR
THE AGE OF COMPLEXITY

Niels Pflaeging/Silke Hermann
Complexitools.
How to (re)vitalize work and make organizations
fit for a complex world
BetaCodex Publishing 2020.
Paperback/eBook. ISBN 978-3-9484710-6-4

WWW.BETACODEXPUBLISHING.COM

149

ABOUT THE AUTHOR

As an advisor, speaker and author, Niels Pflaeging earned a reputation as a highly progressive organizational expert and innovator.
He likes to think of himself as a serious business thinker, but at
the same time as a practitioner who cares about the nitty-gritty
details of business. Niels is founder of the *BetaCodex Network* and
co-founder of *Red42*, an innovation-centric start-up on the fringe of
organizational development and Learning & Development (L&D),
based in Wiesbaden, Germany. As a consultant, he has been helping organizations of all kinds with mastering profound change, for
over 15 years now.

From 2003 to 2007, Niels was a director of the *Beyond Budgeting
Round Table* (BBRT), the think tank that developed the foundational research into what we now call Beta, or the BetaCodex. It
was during his time as a BBRT research director that he discovered
his passion for organizational transformation towards coherent
self-organization. In 2008, after breaking free from the BBRT, Niels
co-founded the BetaCodex Network, an open source movement for
Beta transformation. You can find more about Beta and about the
network on www.betacodex.org.

Essays on Beta, Vol. 1 is Niels´ first collection of essays. It is his 10th
book, overall, and his third to be published in English. Niels´ previous books include the best-seller *Organize for Complexity* (2014)

and *OpenSpace Beta* (2018, with Silke Hermann). Together with Silke, Niels is the creator of concepts such as *OrgPhysics* and *Change-as-Flipping*, and of the open source social technologies *OpenSpace Beta, Cell Structure Design* and *LearningCircles by Red42.*

If you have questions or comments about this book, or if you want to learn more about how to make Beta happen in your organization, or with your clients, then do not hesitate to reach out to Niels.

You can reach him through niels.pflaeging@redforty2.com.
Follow Niels on Twitter: @NielsPflaeging
The Red42 website: www.redforty2.com

THANK YOU!

Niels wishes to thank:

Bjoern Janssen – for translating a couple of texts for this book from German into English – which greatly helped making the book´s concept complete.

Paul Tolchinsky, Steve Holyer, Matt Moersch and Andi Roberts – for reviewing and copy-editing the manuscript.
You guys truly made a difference!

Silke Hermann – for being one of the smartest people in the world, and for walking the talk every day. Also, for creating several of the concepts with me that are laid out in this volume.

My peers in the BetaCodex Network – for joining the movement and for actively contributing to it!

My teachers at school, namely Karin Neugebauer, who taught me to always take responsibility. And to my teachers at university, namely Prof. Dr. Klaus-Peter Wiedmann, who taught me (among other things) that "even the sun has spots."

My parents, Isa-Maria Pflaeging and Bodo Pflaeging – for making it all possible.

CPSIA information can be obtained
at www.ICGtesting.com
Printed in the USA
JSHW051728270920
8121JS00006B/5

9 783948 471002